Libertarianism

Key Concepts in Political Theory

Libertarianism

Eric Mack

Polity

First published in 2018 by Polity Press

Polity Press
65 Bridge Street
Cambridge CB2 1UR, UK

Polity Press
101 Station Landing
Suite 300
Medford, MA 02155, USA

ISBN-13: 978-1-5095-1929-3
ISBN-13: 978-1-5095-1930-9(pb)

A catalogue record for this book is available from the British Library.
Library of Congress Cataloging-in-Publication Data
Names: Mack, Eric, 1946- author.
Title: Libertarianism / Eric Mack.
Description: Cambridge, UK ; Medford, MA : Polity Press, 2018. | Series: Key concepts in political theory | Includes bibliographical references and index.
Identifiers: LCCN 2018002844 (print) | LCCN 2018019786 (ebook) | ISBN 9781509519330 (Epub) | ISBN 9781509519293 (hardback) | ISBN 9781509519309
(pbk.)
Subjects: LCSH: Libertarianism. | Political science--Philosophy.
Classification: LCC JC585 (ebook) | LCC JC585 .M33 2018 (print) | DDC 320.51/2--dc23
LC record available at https://lccn.loc.gov/2018002844

Typeset in 10.5 on 12 pt Sabon
by Fakenham Prepress Solutions, Fakenham, Norfolk NR21 8NL
Printed and bound in Great Britain by CPI Group (UK) Ltd, Croydon

For further information on Polity, visit our website:
politybooks.com

Contents

Further Philosophical Roads to Libertarianism, Online
    chapter available at:
    http://politybooks.com/mack-online-chapter/

Acknowledgments

I wish to thank Mary Sirridge, Doug Den Uyl, Doug Rasmussen, David Schmidtz, and Hillel Steiner for their very helpful feedback on portions of this book, George Owers for his excellent editorial suggestions, and Ian Tuttle for his meticulous copy-editing. I also thank Liberty Fund and the Murphy Institute of Political Economy for their generous support.

For Josh and Sara, Rebekah and Jon, and Rose

1

Introduction

This book is about the stance within political philosophy known as libertarianism. More specifically, it focuses on the key philosophical themes and arguments that have been offered on behalf of libertarianism. I begin this introduction with an explanation of what political libertarianism is. Then I briefly describe the central themes and arguments of libertarian theory that are developed in this book, and where and in what form these themes and arguments are to be found.

Libertarianism is advocacy of individual liberty as the fundamental political norm. An individual's liberty is understood as that individual not being subject to interference by other agents in her doing as she sees fit with her own person and legitimate holdings. Your liberty is violated when, by striking you in the nose, I prevent you from using your face as you choose. Your liberty is not violated when I dodge the punch you aim at me which would otherwise rearrange my nose; for my nose is not part of your person or legitimate holdings. Libertarianism – especially in its more hardcore forms – maintains that respect for one's liberty is the basic moral demand that each individual can make against all other individuals and groups. A bit more precisely, each individual who is not herself violating the principle that liberty is to be respected can demand respect for her liberty from all other individuals and groups. In the name of liberty so understood, each individual who is respectful of others' liberty may demand that she not be murdered, enslaved, maimed, assaulted, robbed, or subjected to extortion through the threat of being murdered, enslaved, maimed, assaulted, or robbed. So stringent is the demand that individuals not be subjected to such morally criminal treatment that coercion is permissible if (but only if) it blocks or nullifies the effects of such violations of liberty.

Libertarians, as we shall see, differ about the justification of this moral requirement that each person's liberty be respected. And they may differ about the precise implications of this requirement. However, libertarians are united in the view that violations of the liberty of liberty-respecting individuals are morally criminal whether it is carried out by individual ruffians or by the agents or high officials of political or legal institutions. As John Locke put it in his *Second Treatise of Government*, "The injury and the crime is equal, whether committed by the wearer of a crown, or some petty villain. The title of the offender, and the number of his followers, make no difference in the offence, unless it be to aggravate it" (1980 [1689]: §176). There are no special "reasons of state" that allow a wearer of a crown or a presidential seal or a police badge to treat any individual in ways that would be recognized as criminal homicide, kidnapping, assault, theft, or extortion if carried out by a freelance lout.

Ruling out "reasons of state" means that state action must be vindicated by ordinary norms of morality – the norms by which we judge whether one individual's treatment of another is morally permissible or impermissible. State actors have no moral privileges. According to the libertarian, at least as a first approximation, ordinary norms of morality require that harmful force or the threat of such force be used against individuals only to defend against or extract restitution for, or to punish initiated force or threat of force, or to enforce compliance with voluntary contracts. Hence, state use of force and the threat of force must also be confined to the functions of defense, restitution, punishment, and the enforcement of contract. Libertarians maintain that the enforcement of a framework within which individuals are secure in their persons, possessions, and contractual arrangements is the key condition for the emergence of a peaceful, tolerant, pluralistic, and prosperous social and economic order. Radical restriction on state action is the key to a flourishing cooperative society.

Hardcore libertarianism rejects all states more extensive than the minimal or night-watchman state which employs coercion solely for the sake of protecting individual liberty. Hardcore anarchist libertarianism rejects even the minimal state on the grounds that in order to be a state it must employ coercion against liberty-respecting individuals. Softer-core versions of libertarianism accept marginal extensions in permissible coercive state action. Such a modest expansion in the scope of acceptable coercive measures may be justified by extending the range of enforceable moral claims that individuals have against their fellows; for example, to claims to assistance when they find themselves in dire straits. Or such an expansion may be based on the view that minor infringements on liberty can be justified if those infringements are necessary to serve some vitally important social condition; for example, the preservation of social peace or maintenance of institutions capable of protecting individuals against major violations of their liberty. As libertarianism becomes softer-core and the small state replaces anarchy or the minimal state as the object of ideological advocacy, libertarianism shades into classical liberalism.

Classical liberals maintain that respect for individual liberty is at least the primary political norm. Moreover, classical liberalism remains united with libertarianism in its insistence that the state and its officials are subject to the same fundamental moral constraints that apply to individuals at large. Classical liberals join libertarians in their willingness to recognize that most of the world historical statesmen of human history have been thieves and murderers writ large. More generally, libertarians and classical liberals are highly suspicious of any proposal to increase the coercive power of the state – and thereby decrease the scope for voluntary action and cooperation – whatever pretext is offered for that aggrandizement. They are united in their threefold opposition to state interference with personal liberty and with economic liberty and all state employment of military force that is not vindicated as strictly necessary for the defense of the liberty of its citizens.[1]

The overall libertarian (and classical liberal) perspective includes normative commitments concerning the separate moral importance of each individual and the ways in which respect for individual freedom is the appropriate response to the importance and value of each individual, undergirding claims about the nature and bases of cooperative social and economic order, and a myriad of more straightforwardly empirical claims about, for example, the systematic benefits of a regime of private property and voluntary contract; the capacity of free individuals and associations to find non-coercive solutions to many of the problems that they face;[2] the capacity of political entrepreneurs to deploy any attractive goal as a device to feather their own nests – often at the expense of those they pretend to serve; and the dangers of state power whether in the hands of dedicated servants of special interests or (worse yet) sincere visionaries. Libertarians conjoin their most basic moral and social theoretic claims with yet more specific empirical and historical contentions about, for example, the beneficial effects of the Industrial Revolution and the expansion of international free trade, the essential role of governmental action in triggering or sustaining various social evils such as racial segregation and economic dislocations, and the generally counter-productive and harmful effects of policies and movements to render people wards of the state. However, these sorts of empirical and historical contentions are beyond the scope of this book, which concentrates on the key philosophical themes and arguments that are supportive of libertarianism.

There are two main philosophical themes that contend for supremacy within libertarian doctrine. There is the natural rights theme, according to which certain deep truths about human beings and their prospective interaction allows us to infer that each person has certain basic ("natural") moral rights that must be respected by all other persons, groups, and institutions. Respect for these rights is taken to lead predictably to mutually advantageous social and economic order. However, those mutually advantageous outcomes are viewed by champions of the natural rights theme as normative icing on the cake. They are reasons to be pleased about people's rights being respected; but the fundamental reason for respecting people's rights is that such respect is morally required by persons' moral standing as bearers of those rights. In contrast, there is the cooperation to mutual advantage theme, according to which general compliance with certain principles of justice engenders a cooperative social and economic order that is advantageous to all of its members. That mutually advantageous outcome is the societal end – the normative cake itself – that calls upon us to abide by those cooperation-inducing principles of justice. Nevertheless, these two approaches are hardly ships that pass in the night. For the restrictions on our conduct that the mutual advantage approach calls upon us to adopt are the same restrictions that the natural rights approach endorses, viz., restrictions against interference with one another's lives, liberties, and legitimately acquired holdings and contractual claims.[3]

Still, not all libertarian theorizing gives explicit pride of place to natural rights or cooperation to mutual advantage. Indeed, there is almost no limit to the moral perspectives upon which someone has sought to ground libertarian political conclusions.[4] A third possible approach that deserves mention is a form of utilitarianism that maintains that the greatest happiness must be pursed indirectly through steadfast compliance with certain constraining moral norms – as it turns out, pretty much the same constraining norms that are celebrated by the natural rights and mutual advantage approaches. Utilitarianism as such asserts that the ultimate standard for assessing a social state is the degree to which the total happiness that obtains in that state exceeds the total unhappiness. Social state S_1 ranks higher than social state S_2 if and only if aggregate happiness in S_1 more exceeds aggregate unhappiness than aggregate happiness exceeds aggregate unhappiness or ill-being in S_2. Without further refinement, such a utilitarianism calls for actions and policies that enhance the aggregate happiness even when those actions and policies coercively impose sacrifices on particular, peaceful and non-offending individuals. The individual is to surrender or be deprived of her life, liberty, or property whenever doing so is truly socially expedient. Conscientious statesmen are always to be alert to opportunities to break a few eggs in order to construct a better social omelet. Such an unrefined, direct utilitarianism is deeply antithetical to the spirit and contentions of libertarianism.

Nevertheless, important utilitarian theorists have maintained that the reasonable form of utilitarianism takes the key to the promotion of overall human happiness to be steadfast reciprocal compliance with norms that are protective of individual liberty – or, more broadly, protective of life, liberty, property, and contract. Such forms of indirect utilitarianism often shade into versions of the mutual advantage perspective because the protection of the liberty of each individual is taken to be essential to the promotion of the greatest aggregate net happiness. For the protection of each individual's liberty is taken to secure each individual's opportunity to advance her own good in ways that do not lessen any other individual's opportunity to promote her own good. A crucial feature of such libertarian-friendly, indirect forms of utilitarianism is that the ultimate "greatest happiness" standard recedes into the background while norms very much like those advocated by natural rights or mutual advantage theorists dominate the moral foreground.

These three philosophical themes are examined and developed in the next three chapters and also in this book's bonus online chapter. In Chapter 2, "Philosophical Antecedents," I flesh out these themes historically by providing accounts of John Locke's natural rights doctrine, David Hume's account of the principles of justice as the norms that facilitate cooperation to mutual advantage, John Stuart Mill's contention that the path to the greatest happiness consists in principled respect for individual security and liberty, and Herbert Spencer's parallel, but broader and more fully libertarian contention that the attainment of the greatest happiness requires replacing the pursuit of expediency with strict regard for the rights that follow from the principle of equal liberty. Chapter 3, "Libertarian Foundations," and Chapter 4, "Economic Justice and Property Rights," explore the core claims of the two theorists from the later decades of the twentieth century who are most important for libertarian doctrine, Robert Nozick and F. A. Hayek. Chapter 3 provides an account of Nozick's articulation and defense of the Lockean natural rights theme in *Anarchy, State, and Utopia*, Hayek's Millian indirect utilitarian defense of liberty in his *The Constitution of Liberty*, and Hayek's more Humean focus on the justice of the norms that facilitate cooperation to mutual advantage in his *Law, Legislation, and*

Liberty. Chapter 4 provides an account of Nozick's historical entitlement conception of justice in holdings and his critique of standard doctrines of distributive justice, and Hayek's critique of "social justice" and his arguments on behalf a free market economic order.

The bonus online chapter, "Further Philosophical Roads to Libertarianism," – which is available on Polity's website at http://politybooks.com/mack-online-chapter/ – examines Hillel Steiner's development and defense of a "left-libertarian" doctrine that in significant ways follows up on Herbert Spencer's early *Social Statics*, Loren Lomasky's *Persons, Rights, and the Moral Community*, which offers a Humean-contractarian defense of basic moral rights; Douglas Rasmussen and Douglas Den Uyl's defense of libertarian political conclusions on the basis of their neo-Aristotelian account of the nature and value of human flourishing; and David Schmidtz's sophisticated indirect utilitarian libertarian-leaning doctrine. Finally, Chapter 5, "Objections: Internal and External," begins with the internal debate between anarchist libertarians, libertarians who defend a minimal state that abjures taxation, and libertarians who allow taxation in order to fund rights-protective activities. This chapter then turns to three of the innumerable critiques by opponents of libertarians. I provide accounts and assessments of John Rawls' critique of Nozickian libertarianism, Liam Murphy and Thomas Nagel's objection to libertarianism's characteristic appeal to pre-institutional moral rights, and G. A. Cohen's efforts to display the attractiveness and feasibility of an egalitarian and (at least in spirit) anti-capitalist economic order.

Throughout this book, I seek to offer critical but sympathetic accounts of central philosophical arguments that are offered in support of libertarian (or near-libertarian) conclusions and to discuss important philosophical criticisms of libertarian theses in ways that further illuminate the libertarian stance. My goal is to advance the reader's appreciation for these themes within libertarian theorizing. Although I have not been bashful about citing a good number of my own philosophical essays, I have not taken the composition of this book as an occasion for systematically presenting my own best case for libertarian conclusions – including my own views about how directly one may translate one's theoretical conclusions within political philosophy into reasonable proposals for change in our complex and tangled world.

2
Philosophical Antecedents

Introduction

This chapter offers accounts of John Locke's articulation of the natural rights theme, David Hume's articulation of the cooperation to mutual advantage theme (along with allied ideas offered by Adam Smith), and John Stuart Mill and Herbert Spencer's articulations of the indirect utilitarian theme. My goal here is not to provide episodes in the history of libertarian political thought. Rather, it is to flesh out philosophical themes that are central to libertarian and classical liberal theorizing – including the theorizing that will be examined in the next three chapters – whether or not each of their expositors should be classified as a libertarian or classical liberal.

Locke on Natural Rights, Political Society, Resistance, and Toleration

The two most important seventeenth-century English defenses of unlimited political authority, those authored by Robert Filmer and Thomas Hobbes, were composed around the time of the English Civil Wars and were still, in their somewhat divergent ways, the primary vindications of the absolutist position in the decade leading up to the Glorious Revolution of 1688. John Locke's two most important works in political philosophy, *Two Treatises of Government* and *A Letter Concerning Toleration*, were composed in this tumultuous decade. The *Two Treatises* was largely written between 1679 and 1683 as both a critique of absolutism and as support for the increasing extra-legal opposition to Charles II that was led by Locke's patron, the Earl of Shaftesbury. The *Letter* was written in 1685 while Locke was in hiding in Holland – on the lam for his association with revolutionary activities in England in 1679–83. Both works were published in England in 1689 after Locke's return following the Glorious Revolution. I will begin with the doctrine of the *Two Treatises* and then turn to the *Letter*.

Locke's *First Treatise* – most of which was lost during Locke's exile – was a detailed critique of Filmer's defense of monarchical authority. Locke presents his own positive doctrine in the *Second Treatise*. Locke frequently employs the traditional language of the "Law of Nature," but he takes the core substance of the Law of Nature to consist in the moral rights possessed by all individuals. Locke takes these rights to define morally protected domains within which individuals may do as they see fit. Locke rejects the Hobbesian view that freedom is a matter of being under no moral constraints and, hence, being morally at liberty to do *whatever* one pleases. For, if one is subject to no moral constraints, others also will be under no such constraints and, hence, they will be free to domineer over one whenever it suits their humor to do so. That can hardly be a state of freedom. Instead, freedom requires we each be subject to norms that preclude "restraint and violence from others" – norms that preclude infringement upon one's "person, actions, possessions, and [one's] whole property." While these norms provide one with protection against the arbitrary will of others, to be subject to these norms is not to be subject to anyone's arbitrary will (1980: §57).

The keynote claim of the *Second Treatise* is that each person possesses a natural moral right to freedom – a natural right to live one's own life in accord with one's own choices. This fundamental right is articulated in terms of a number of somewhat more specific first-order rights, viz., the right to dispose of one's own body, faculties, and efforts as one sees fit and the right to acquire holdings in extra-personal objects which one may use as one sees fit. Correlative to each person's natural rights are each other persons' natural obligations "... not, unless it be to do justice on an offender, to take away, or impair the life, or what tends to the preservation of the life, the liberty, health, limb, or goods of another" (1980: §6). A further aspect of our natural right to freedom is our right that others not violate their contractual agreements with us. "[P]romises and compacts" made in the state of nature are binding on us because "truth and keeping of faith belongs to men as men" (1980: §14). In addition, all persons possess second-order natural rights to defend themselves against violations of their first-order rights and to extract restitution from and to punish those who have violated their rights (1980: §10–§12).

It is often said that Locke simply asserts these natural rights or asserts that God has decreed them. This is a serious misreading. Throughout his life Locke did hold that the law of nature counts as *law* and as *obligatory* because of God's authoritative endorsement of it (1959: 473, 474). Nevertheless, the rights that God wills that we abide by are grounded in our nature; and they can only be known through an investigation of our nature. As Locke puts it in his early (1663–4) *Essays on the Law of Nature,*

> since man has been made such as he is, equipped with reason and his other faculties and destined for this mode of life, there necessarily result from his inborn constitution some definite duties for him, which cannot be other than they are ... [H]e has made man such that these duties of his necessarily follow from his very nature ... [N]atural law stands and falls together with the nature of man as it is at present. (1997b: 125, 126)

The law of nature is "the permanent rule of morals" because it is "firmly rooted in the soil of human nature." Locke's claims about the rights of individuals, the nature of the political institutions they have reason to adopt, and the grounds for resistance against unjust state action are largely detached from his theological contentions that God created us and wills that we respect the rights that are rooted in our human nature.

Almost all of Locke's argumentation in the *Second Treatise* on behalf of natural rights rests on two normatively seminal facts about our inborn condition. The first of these is that each individual pursues his own happiness and that this pursuit of happiness is rational. In his *An Essay Concerning Human Understanding*, Locke says that, while all human happiness is good, each individual naturally and reasonably pursues his own happiness. "All other good, however great in reality or appearance, excites not a man's desires who looks not on it to make a part of that happiness wherewith he, in his present thoughts, can satisfy himself" (1959: 341). Locke makes clear that he is affirming each individual's pursuit of *personal* happiness in a fragment written shortly before the publication of the *Two Treatises*.

> 'Tis a man's proper business to seek happiness and avoid misery. ... I will therefore make it my business to seek satisfaction and delight and avoid uneasiness and disquiet and to have as much of the one and as little of the other as may be. But here I must have a care I mistake not, for if I prefer a short pleasure to a lasting one, 'tis plain I cross my own happiness. (1997d: 296)

In the *Second Treatise*, Locke focuses on the crucial, necessary condition of individual happiness, viz., self-preservation and more specifically yet on the crucial *interpersonally* necessary condition for self-preservation, viz. freedom. Freedom is what we need *from other people* if we are to attain self-preservation and happiness (1980: §17).

The second normatively seminal fact about human beings is that we all have the same fundamental moral standing. We are naturally in a state of moral equality,

> wherein all the power and jurisdiction is reciprocal, no one having more than another; there being nothing more evident, than that creatures of the same species and rank, promiscuously born to all the same advantages of nature, and the use of the same faculties, should also be equal one amongst another without subordination or subjection. (1980: §4)

We are all "equal and independent" beings "sharing all in one community of nature." Both these claims come into play in the various ways in which Locke supports his claim that "reason ... teaches all mankind ... that being all *equal and independent*, no one ought to harm another in his life, health, liberty, or possessions" (1980: §6).

The first of Locke's arguments for a natural right to freedom is the generalization argument. It begins with Locke reiterating "[t]his *equality* of men by nature" (1980: §5). Locke then provides a long passage in which Richard Hooker asserts that, if one makes a claim to be loved by others, one must recognize their like claim to one's love for them. Since Locke himself is not proposing that we each have a right to be loved and an obligation to love, the point of the Hooker passage must be to illustrate the principle of generalization; any claim that one makes for oneself against others, one must grant to all others of the same moral status. For Locke, the crucial claim that is rational for each person to make against others is the claim to freedom from interference. Since each rationally makes this claim against others, each is rationally required to affirm every other person's right to freedom from interference.

The second of Locke's arguments is the non-subordination argument. Absent some special agreement with or provocation by another, one is justified in "harm[ing] another in his life, health, liberty, or possessions" (1980: §6) only if this other person is naturally subordinate to one. However, it is false that other persons are naturally subordinate to one. Human beings do not exist for "one another's pleasure: and being furnished with like faculties, sharing all in one community of nature, there cannot be supposed any such *subordination* among us, that may authorize us to destroy one another, as if we were made for one another's uses" (1980: §6, original emphasis). Since each person is an "equal and independent" being, absent special agreement or provocation, the subordination of that person to one's own purposes wrongs that individual.

One further Lockean argument deserves mention: the preservation of mankind argument. According to Locke, each of us is "*bound to preserve himself*" (1980: §6). I am bound to preserve myself and I need to recognize that each other human being is "by like reason" bound to preserve himself. Locke then proclaims that each person, "when his own preservation comes not in competition, ought he, as much as he can, *to preserve the rest of mankind*" (1980: §6). It sounds as though Locke is saying that, when it does not endanger one's own preservation, one is bound to devote oneself to the preservation of others. Yet, when Locke parses his call for preserving the rest of mankind, he says that this requires one "... not, unless it be to do justice to an offender, take away, or impair the life, or what tends to the preservation of the life, the liberty, health, limb, or goods of another" (1980: §6). And in the next sentence he says that to preserve the rest of mankind is to be "restrained from invading others rights, and from doing hurt to one another" (1980: §7). So, the most plausible reading of the "preserve the rest of mankind argument" is that, while one's appropriate response to the fact that one is bound to preserve oneself is for one to seek one's self-preservation, one's appropriate response to the fact that *another* is bound to preserve *himself* is *not to hinder* that other person's pursuit of his self-preservation. One's happiness provides one with an end that one has reason to *promote* while others having like ends of their own provides one with reason to be *constrained* in one's conduct toward them.

Locke's arguments for a natural right to do as one sees fit with one's person, one's liberty, and one's possessions bypass the question of what makes a possession legitimate and, hence, *properly* within the possessor's domain of freedom. Locke turns to this question in his famous chapter "Of Property" which begins with the rejection of the idea that the earth is originally jointly owned by all of mankind. If the earth were originally jointly owned, every individual's use or appropriation of any raw material would require the unanimous consent of all of mankind. However, such consent has never and will never be given. "If such a consent as that was necessary, man had starved, notwithstanding the plenty God had given him" (1980: §28). Since the premise that the earth is originally jointly owned leads to the conclusion that all morally upright persons must sit still and starve, this premise must be mistaken. Instead, the earth must be originally unowned. This opens the way for individuals to use the raw material of the earth without first asking leave of all of mankind and for individuals to acquire property in portions of the earth "without any express compact of all the commoners" (1980: §25).

Locke had argued in the *First Treatise* (*FT* 1960: §86–§88), that since each person has a right to pursue his happiness and self-preservation and the sustained, purposeful use and transformation of raw material is crucial to this pursuit, individuals must have a right to use and acquire unowned raw material; therefore, there must be some procedure that gives rise to rightful possession. In the *Second Treatise* he provides his famous labor-mixing account of just initial acquisition. Since "every man has a *property* in his own person ... The *labour* of his body, and the *work* of his hands, we may say, are properly his" (1980: §27). Persons acquire private property rights by mixing their labor with bits of unowned material. Locke is not saying that one gathers up a cup or a shovelful of one's labor and literally mixes this with an acre of raw land or ten kilos of iron ore. Rather, he is talking about one's industrious transformation of some raw material for the sake of some intended ongoing use or project. Through the purposive mixing of his labor with some raw material, an individual invests his productive capacities and energies in the resulting object. If another agent, without the consent of the labor investor, then takes possession of that object or precludes the investor from making use of that object, that other agent deprives the investor of a portion of his productive capacities and energies and, thereby, violates the investor's self-propriety. Just as the conscription of a man's labor for one's own purposes is a type of rights-violating enslavement of that man, so too it is a type of enslavement to take possession of or control over an object in which a man has invested his labor without his consent. In addition, Locke holds that ownership over justly held objects can be transferred through the voluntary consent of the antecedent owners.

Nevertheless, Locke endorses two restrictions on legitimately acquired holdings. The first restriction is that one will not have a just title to what one has acquired through labor investment or free exchange if that holding will spoil in one's possession. However, this restriction has little bite since only irrational people will labor or trade for goods that will spoil in their possession; and, once money comes into existence, one will always be able to exchange goods that will perish in one's possession for non-perishable coins. The second and more important restriction is that one will not have a just title to goods that one has acquired through labor investment or voluntary exchange if one's possession will not leave others with "enough, and as good" (1980: §27) for their use or acquisition. Locke is not saying that *equal* amounts of raw material have to be left for others. Rather, each person has a claim against being "straitened" by the acquisitions of others (1980: §36).

Locke holds that this proviso is readily satisfied before money comes into existence. If money did not exist, the *"rule of propriety, (viz.)* that every man should have as much as he could make use of, should still hold in the world, without straitening any body, since there is land enough in the world to suffice double the inhabitants" (1980: §36). Also, those who become cultivators – and, hence, owners – of land use less land than they have used as hunter-gathers. Thus, their acquisition of private property in land releases more land for the use of others (1980: §37). However, the appearance of money vastly changes matters. For, money, both as a means of exchange and a store of value, greatly encourages increased production for profitable trade. In turn, this encourages more extensive appropriation of raw material for the sake of production for trade, and this more extensive appropriation may well leave some people without as much opportunity to use or appropriate *raw materials* as they would have had if all of the earth had remained in the commons (1980: §48, §49).

Locke's official and weak argument at this point is that the developments that follow the introduction of money will not violate the "enough, and as good" proviso because that proviso will have been repealed through everyone's agreement to the existence of money. That argument is weak because money does not in fact arise through agreement and, even if it did, not everyone who ends up worse off in terms of opportunity to use or acquire raw material will have been a party to that agreement. There is, however, a better and very important argument that is lurking just below the surface of Locke's bad argument. That argument turns on the reason that Locke takes everyone to have for agreeing to the existence of money. That reason is that all individuals will at least reasonably expect to be net gainers because of the vast expansion of productive economic activity that comes in the wake of the introduction of money – along with the establishment of "laws of liberty to secure protection and encouragement to the honest industry of mankind" (1980: §42).

This facilitation of human industry – of the creation and employment of human capital – greatly increases the size and the vibrancy of economic life. Indeed, it is specifically through the introduction of more productive forms of labor that economic wealth is enhanced. For *"labour makes the far greatest part of the value* of things we enjoy in this world: and the ground which produces the [raw] materials, is scarce to be reckoned in, as any, or at most, but a very small part of it" (1980: §42). Since wealth arises from labor which can be expanded and made more productive, one person's economic gain is apt to favor, rather than impede, the economic gains of others. Moreover, the enhanced scope and vigor of productive economic activity is likely to make everyone a net gainer in economic opportunity – even those for whom less *raw* material remains available for use or appropriation.

Locke begins his account of justifiable political authority with a picture of human existence in a state of nature, that is, in the absence of political institutions. The key idea of state of nature theorizing is to determine what problems (if any) would exist in the absence of political authority and to posit that rational individuals would grant to political rulers only the sort of authority needed to solve those problems. Locke's picture of the state of nature differs sharply from Hobbes' depiction for two reasons. First, contrary to Hobbes, Locke holds that "The *state of nature* has a law of nature to govern it" (1980: §6), which is at least primarily a matter of individuals possessing by nature rights over themselves, their liberty, their labor and, through the exercise of their natural rights, particular acquired rights to property and contractual compliance. Second, Locke presumes that in the absence of centralized political enforcement of these rights, individuals will to some significant degree be disposed to abide by one another's rights.

Nevertheless, in the state of nature there will be some intentional or negligent violations of rights and, especially as more complex forms of property and contracts arise, there will be honest disputes about whether particular actions or omissions are infringements upon rights. In addition to this, there is a tendency for people engaged in disputes to be biased on their own behalf and to be aware of this bias in others. Even if an individual arrives at a sound judgment about whose rights have been violated by whom and what the proper restitution and punishment should be, the soundness of this judgment may not be known to others and the power to enforce the judgment may not exist. As a result, in the state of nature, the enjoyment of one's rights will be "very unsafe, very insecure" (1980: §123). Locke tells us that, to secure safety for "the mutual preservation of their lives, liberties, and estates, which I call by the general name, property" (1980: §123), individuals consensually form political society. And, in turn, political society establishes a political order with three crucial functions: the clear articulation and promulgation of laws – "which are only so far right, as they are founded on the law of nature" (1980: §12); the appointment of known and impartial judges; and the marshalling of sufficient power to enforce just law and judicial decisions.

With one exception, those who form political society cede to it only their second-order rights of defense, restitution, and punishment. Indeed, because each individual is bound to preserve himself and, hence, to preserve his freedom, no one can cede more than these rights. To think that people seeking to avoid the dangers of the state of nature would put themselves under an unrestricted Hobbesian sovereign is "to think, that men are so foolish, that they take care to avoid what mischiefs may be done them by *pole-cats* or *foxes*; but are content, nay, think it safety, to be devoured by *lions*" (1980: §93). The one exception is that one's entrance into political society also includes consent to taxation to fund the sanctioned functions of government (1980: §140). Indeed, this is the crucial element of consent. For consent to be subject to rightful defensive, restitutive, or retributive force by an established state is no more necessary than consent to be subject to such force in the state of nature. In contrast, state taxation that is not consented to is on a par with state of nature robbery. "[F]or I truly have no *property* in that, which another by right takes from me, when he pleases, against my consent" (1980: §138). The real problem for Locke that arises in connection with his attempt to provide a social contract justification for political society and the state is that consent has not in fact been given for the state's taxation of its subjects and, hence, on Lockean grounds that taxation is theft.

The final two chapters of the *Second Treatise* are devoted to defending forceful resistance by individuals and by political society at large against overreaching state power. Locke's core premise here is that all political rulers – be they monarchs or parliaments – remain subject to the basic moral constraints imposed by the law of nature. They are charged to protect and must not themselves infringe upon their subjects' rights of life, liberty, and estate. In addition, existing rulers are bound to preserve the constitutional order that is created to serve those rights. Individuals and political society do agree to public authorities drawing the natural law closer by providing clear and known codifications of its strictures (1980: §135). If more fine-grained enacted laws and their administration can reasonably be construed as satisfying those strictures, members of political society are bound to abide by them even if they are not precisely the enacted laws or modes of administration which this or that member would most favor. Nevertheless, when legislation or executive action clearly violates a subject's retained rights or the contract that exists between political society and its chosen ruler, forcible resistance is justified. That the present ruler has crossed the line is most clear when "a long train of abuses, prevarications and artifices" (1980: §225) make visible a design to act contrary to the retained rights of individuals or to his contractual obligations to political society.

Forcible resistance to injustice "may occasion disorder and bloodshed." But what is the alternative? "I desire it may be considered, what a kind of peace there will be in the world, which consists only in violence and rapine; and which is to be maintained only for the benefit of robbers and oppressors" (1980: §228). Since rulers remain subject to the basic constraints of the law of nature, Locke has no hesitation about saying that they are criminals when they clearly break through those constraints. Indeed, one of the most strikingly libertarian aspects of Locke's thought is his obvious hatred of any double standard that whitewashes the crimes of established rulers.

> The injury and the crime is equal, whether committed by the wearer of a crown, or some petty villain. The title of the offender, and the number of his followers, make no difference in the offence, unless it be to aggravate it. The difference is, great robbers punish little ones, to keep them in their obedience; but the great ones are rewarded with laurels and triumphs, because they are too big for the weak hands of justice in this world, and have the power in their possession, which should punish offenders. (1980: §176)

There is more than a hint here of the radical libertarian contention that the state's enforcement of its monopoly on the use of force in society amounts to the enforcement of its monopoly on the commission of crime.

It is crucial to recall that libertarianism stands as much for "personal" liberty as "economic" liberty. The essential connection between these stances is brought out by two features of Locke's *A Letter Concerning Toleration*. First, the *Letter* both defends religious freedom as an implication of the Second Treatise's general defense of private property, freedom of contract, and radical limits on state authority. Second, it is clear that Locke also views religious toleration as the prime exemplar of rightful human freedom. Freedom starts with religious toleration and the repudiation of the state's pretense of authority over the individual's pursuit of salvation; and it generalizes into Locke's radical critique of overreaching coercive power. In *A Letter*, this critique extends to coercive efforts to suppress sinful actions that are not prejudicial to the rights of others (1983: 44) and to coercive paternalist efforts to protect people from their own mistakes (1983: 34, 35).

The essence of toleration is minding one's own business and allowing others to mind theirs. Toleration requires the decentralization – de-politicalization – of decision-making authority. Such decentralization requires the recognition of distinct domains – distinct spheres of action – over which distinct individuals (or the associations that they voluntarily form) have authority. Within a tolerant social order, the role of legitimate coercive institutions is not to enforce collective judgments about how people should worship or marry or medicate themselves but, rather, to enforce people's rights to do as they see fit with themselves and their just possessions. These points are illustrated by Locke through his consideration of a dispute between those who believe that the sacrifice of a calf will be "well-pleasing to God" (1983: 42) and those who believe it will be displeasing to God. According to Locke, the dispute about the use of the calf should not be settled by a political judgment about whether the sacrifice of calves is pleasing or displeasing to God. Rather, the dispute should be settled by identifying "whose Calf it is" (1983: 42), that is, which party has the right to dispose as he sees fit of this particular calf. Suppose this particular calf belongs to the party who believes that its sacrifice will be well-pleasing to God. Then the other party must allow the sacrifice to be performed; that other party must *tolerate* the sacrifice on the grounds that the other party has authority over this calf. But that party need not endorse that sacrifice or the judgment that the sacrifice will be pleasing to God.

There is one argument that beautifully conveys Locke's deeply libertarian view that social disorder and strife arise not from freedom but, rather, from deprivations of freedom. Locke considers the argument that religious dissidents are known to be threats to peace and order because they are always meeting in secret and grumbling about their persecution. Hence, their suppression or extirpation is justified. Locke asks his readers to imagine that black-haired or gray-eyed people suffered the same sorts of restrictions and injuries that are imposed on religious dissenters. They too would tend to gather in secret and grumble about their lot and even conspire to overturn their persecutors. "[T]hese men, growing weary of the Evils under which they labour, should in the end think it lawful for them to resist Force with Force, and to defend their natural Rights" (1983: 55). But what is the true source of the danger? "[T]here is one only thing which gathers People into Seditious Commotions, and that is Oppression" (1983: 52). "It is not the diversity of Opinions (which cannot be avoided), but the refusal of Toleration to those that are of different Opinions (which might have been granted), that has produced all the Bustles and Wars, that have been in the Christian World, upon the account of Religion" (1983: 55).[1]

Hume on Principles for Cooperation to Mutual Advantage

David Hume is generally seen as a philosophical opponent of Lockean political theory – partly on the basis of his critique of social contract theory and his disavowal of traditional natural law even in its natural rights version (Hume 1985). Be that as it may, Hume's account of the connections among property, justice, and social cooperation is a key moment in the development of classical liberal and libertarian thought. Here I focus on Hume's exposition in Book III ("Of Morals") of his *A Treatise of Human Nature* (2000 [1740]). In a famous passage, Hume says that, compared to all other species of animals, human beings are very poorly endowed by nature with the means to satisfy their natural needs and passions. There are species that have very elaborate needs – such as lions who need to consume large amounts of meat to stay alive – but who also have very elaborate natural means to satisfy these needs, for example, great speed, sharp claws, and powerful jaws. And there are species that have very modest natural means to satisfy their needs – such as sheep who can only ramble along and get their mouths down to the ground – but who have only modest needs, for example for mouthfuls of grass. For species within each of these categories there is a nice fit between their natural needs and their natural means for satisfying those needs. Human beings are the exception. We have elaborate natural needs for food, clothing, shelter, and so on, but few natural powers to provide for them. As Hume puts it, "In man alone, this unnatural conjunction of infirmity, and of necessity, may be observ'd in its greatest perfection" (2000: 312). Human beings can overcome this disadvantage only through cooperative interaction. "'Tis by society alone he is able to supply his defect" (2000: 312).

By "society" Hume has in mind a network of cooperative economic interaction; and, he holds that the existence of such cooperative interaction depends upon people generally complying with, and being expected to comply with, certain principles of justice. However, Hume denies that there is a natural desire to comply with these principles. Our only natural motivations are our selfishness and our limited generosity. And, in their untempered form, both of these are barriers to cooperation. My natural desire to advance my own interests *and* my natural desire to advance the welfare of my family and friends will dispose me to seek out opportunities to seize the possessions of others that will satisfy my needs or those of my family or friends. Others' similar dispositions to seize my possessions will be reinforced by their diminished incentive to produce goods for themselves. And their reinforced focus on plundering me will strengthen my own resolve to advance my interests and those of my family and friends by seizing whatever goods others have managed to produce or seize.

The first principle of justice that enables us to escape from this anti-cooperative quagmire and at least achieve peaceful co-existence is "the stability of possessions," which forbids the seizure of other people's holdings. General compliance with this principle assures individuals that they will enjoy the fruits of their own labor *and* that they had better engage in productive labor because the option of seizing the fruits of others' labor has been ruled out. The anticipation of this compliance enormously increases everyone's incentive to live by production and not by predation. Still, we can all do better than autarkic co-existence. If each person (or household or nation) labors fruitfully on the material resources immediately at hand, "persons and possessions must often be very ill adjusted" (2000: 330). One person (or household or nation) will produce lots of corn – much more than she (or it) can consume – while another person (or household or nation) will produce lots of herring – much more than she (or it) can consume. We can adjust possessions to persons through voluntary trade. However, our unconstrained self-love and localized benevolence will dispose us to seize the possessions that others have acquired through trade. And our expectation of such seizures will stymie mutually beneficial exchange.

What saves us from this anti-cooperative quagmire is our understanding that we will each be better off if we comply with a second rule – a rule that allows the consensual transfer of possessions and forbids the non-consensual seizure of goods that are acquired through such transfers. Thus, Hume maintains that stability of possession must be supplemented with "the translation of property by consent" (2000: 330).

Still, the rules of the stability of possession and the transference of property "are not sufficient to render [men] as serviceable to each other, as by nature they are fitted to become" (2000: 334). Many mutually beneficial exchanges cannot take place at one point in time because the goods or services to be exchanged will not be available or needed at the same time. Our untempered self-interest and localized benevolence dispose us to try to induce others to deliver goods or services to us today and to evade the payment that we have promised to make next year. And the prospect of such violations of agreements undermines temporally extended trades that would be mutually gainful. This final anti-cooperative quagmire is overcome by the addition of a third rule, "the obligation of promises," which requires that each agent fulfill her promises or contracts. I will help you harvest your crop in June if and only if I have an assured expectation that you will fulfill your promise to help me with my crop in August.

Although Hume labels these three rules "Laws of Nature," he denies that they are natural in the sense of springing from our original passions. Instead, action in accord with these Laws of Nature derives from our understanding that our separate and partial ends will best be advanced in a world in which there is general compliance with all three of these rules. Neither moralists nor politicians "give a new direction to those natural passions;" but they can "teach us that we can better satisfy our appetites in an oblique and artificial manner, than by their headlong and impetuous motion" (2000: 334). We each come to value general compliance with these rules because we each come to see that such compliance is conducive to our own good and to the good of those for whom we especially care. For Hume, cooperation does not require "correcting the selfishness and ingratitude of men" (2000: 334). Rather, the principles of justice enable us to live at peace and positively to cooperate to mutual advantage with an enormous range of people who do not share our personal goals. Single acts of justice – such as returning a wallet that another has unknowingly dropped or reciprocally fulfilling a contract – may seem to be contrary to the actor's (or the public's) interests. However, this is only if one focuses on the action's immediate costs.

> [T]his momentary ill is amply compensated by the steady prosecution of the rule, and by the peace and order, which establishes society. And even every individual person must find himself a gainer, on ballancing the account; since without justice, society must immediately dissolve, and every one must fall into that savage and solitary condition, which is infinitely worse than the worst situation that can possibly be suppos'd in society. (2000: 319)

Still, for Hume, our motivating sentiments do evolve in a certain way. Through sympathy we acquire an *artificial* sentiment on behalf of justice and against injustice. This development is necessary because the combination of our natural passions and our understanding may not suffice to engender compliance with the cooperative rules when the circle of people with whom we interact grows larger. "[W]hen society has become numerous, and has encreas'd to a tribe or nation, this interest [in rule compliance] is more remote; nor do men so readily perceive, that disorder and confusion follow upon every breach of these rules, as in a more narrow and contracted society" (2000: 320). Even within an extended social order, one's self-love and localized benevolence will in fact always be best served by reciprocal compliance with the principles of justice. However, in many particular cases, the damage to one's interests that will derive from the "disorder and confusion" occasioned by one's non-compliance will not be readily perceived. Thus, these passions may combine with our short-sightedness to induce counterproductive defections.

Fortunately, this short-sightedness is counterbalanced by sympathy through which we share in everyone else's "uneasiness" about being subject to unjust conduct (2000: 320–1). This Humean sympathy does not redirect our actions toward the promotion of the interests of distant individuals. Rather, it reinforces our disposition to abide by the principles of justice and sustains our expectation of reciprocal compliance with these norms in more extended social orders. Sympathy adds additional motivational force to our disposition to abide by the norms that facilitate cooperation to mutual advantage. Ultimately, it is this facilitation of cooperation to mutual advantage that recommends these rules to us.

In *The Wealth of Nations* (1776) (Smith 1981), Adam Smith echoes Hume's point that human beings especially need the assistance of one another but are not likely to get that assistance from the benevolence of strangers (1981: 26). Smith also agrees that, when norms of respect for property, trade, and contract are well-entrenched, each person's self-love and localized benevolence will lead him to serve the interests of others.

> It is not from the benevolence of the butcher, the brewer, or the baker, that we expect our dinner, but from their regard to their own interest. We address ourselves, not to their humanity, but to their self-love, and never talk to them of our own necessities but of their advantages.[2] (1981: 27)

One's beneficial cooperation does not depend on ultimate concern for the ends of others. Indeed, individuals participate in vast networks of cooperation without having knowledge of the particular ends of other participants – or even knowledge of who the other cooperating parties are (1981: 22). We can coordinate with one another peacefully and to mutual advantage through "the obvious and simple system of natural liberty," which leaves each individual "perfectly free to pursue his own interest in his own chosen way ... as long as he does not violate the laws of justice" (1981: 687).[3] These laws of justice channel or regularize our pursuit of our own ends and others' pursuit of their own ends in such a way that we each best serve our interests by way of serving one another's interests. The genius of the simple system of natural liberty is that it enables us to live together in mutually beneficial ways without our having to surrender our separate and distinctive goals. Each "intends only his own gain, and he is in this, as in many other cases, led by an invisible hand to promote an end which was no part of his intention" (1981: 456).

Mill on the Utilitarian Case for Liberty

Natural rights doctrine remained influential throughout the eighteenth century. It found its most radiant moment in the opening passages of the American Declaration of Independence. It still powerfully influenced the abolitionist movement and the post-Civil War amendments to the United States Constitution.[4] Yet theoretical advocates of natural rights were few and far between in the nineteenth century. Hume's disavowal of Lockean natural rights and social contract theory was followed by Jeremy Bentham's attack on natural rights as "nonsense on stilts."[5] In the mind of Bentham (1748–1832) and many others, utilitarianism needed to take up the mantle of liberalism that natural rights doctrine was incapable of bearing. In this and the next section, I discuss two thinkers – both of whom are thought of as champions of classical liberalism (or even libertarianism) – who endorse utilitarianism as their most fundamental principle and then struggle to remold utilitarianism so it yields a principled endorsement of individual liberty.

According to Mill, utilitarianism endorses "the Greatest Happiness Principle" according to which "actions are right in proportion as they tend to promote happiness, wrong as they tend to produce the reverse of happiness" (2000: 14). A bit more precisely, the Greatest Happiness Principle states that the right action is the action that will yield the greatest balance of happiness over unhappiness (or the smallest balance of unhappiness over happiness) of all the actions that are available to one. To determine which action is the right one to perform, one must survey the outcome in terms of happiness and unhappiness for each member of one's society (or for all human beings or even for all sentient creatures) and identify the outcome that has the best balance of happiness over unhappiness. The action that has the best overall outcome is – indeed, must be – the right action. One acts wrongly when one acts in a way that does not yield the optimal outcome.

Within utilitarianism, ends rule the roost. Indeed, at the very foundation of utilitarian thought is the supposition that, in the final analysis, all actions are for the sake of ends and (it seems) rules or principles are to be followed insofar, and only insofar, as doing so best serves the sanctified ends (2000: 8). Of course, the ends of actual human beings are distinct and various. Most people are strongly oriented to the advancement of their own well-being and to the well-being of particular other individuals with whom they have ties of family, friendship, or common conviction. Different types of achievements or experiences contribute to or constitute the well-being of diverse persons and the well-being of the individuals cared about by those diverse persons. A common theme in Locke and Hume and the theorists we will consider in the next three chapters – including the bonus online chapter – is that the way to deal with this pervasive and acceptable plurality of ends is to require individuals to abide by certain constraining rules – rules that insure peace and encourage productive endeavors and trade to mutual advantage among these "equal and independent" agents.

With its focus on a single, comprehensive *summum bonum*, utilitarianism seems to be committed to a fundamentally different way of dealing with the plurality of distinct individual ends. This alternative way is the redirection of individuals from activity in the service of their distinct personal ends to conduct for the sake of the common end of maximum net happiness. The pursuit of distinct private ends is not so much to be reconciled as transcended.

> [T]he happiness which forms the utilitarian standard of what is right in conduct, is not the agent's own happiness, but that of all concerned. As between his own happiness and that of others, utilitarianism requires him to be as strictly impartial as a disinterested and benevolent spectator. (2000: 26)

Education and opinion need (in Hume's phrase) to "new-mould the human mind" so, that, for each individual, there will be "an indissoluable association between his own happiness and the good of the whole" (2000: 26). Each individual's character should be so modified that,

> not only may he be unable to conceive the possibility of happiness to himself, consistently with conduct opposed to the general good, but also that a direct impulse to promote

the general good may be in every individual one of the habitual motives of action, and the sentiments connected therewith may fill a large and prominent place in every human being's sentient existence. (2000: 26)

Of course, some people may not be able to derive personal happiness from the promotion of the general happiness. When they are faced with a choice between the two, utilitarianism calls for the sacrifice of the former. In those cases, "All honour to those who can abnegate for themselves the personal enjoyment of life, when by such renunciation they contribute worthily to increase the amount of happiness in the world" (2000: 25). There seems to be no room within utilitarianism for individual rights or principles of justice on the basis of which the distinct lives and pursuits of individuals are shielded from the demands of the *summum bonum*. Rather, conflict among individuals will be avoided and desirable social order will be attained by inducing each individual to march in step to the drum beat of general utility.

Yet, since Mill wants to support individualism and freedom, he denies that utilitarianism calls for the conscription of individuals into the service of the general happiness. In the final chapter of *Utilitarianism*, he rejects such conscription in the name of each individual's moral right to security. Security is a condition that "no human being can possibly do without; on it we depend for all our immunity from evil." It is the "most indispensable of all necessities, after physical nutriment" (2000: 68). Yet why should society protect everyone's security rather than sometimes sacrificing the security of some for the greater good of others – perhaps for the good of their security? Mill tells us that, "To have a right ... is, I conceive, to have something which society ought to defend me in the possession of. If the objector goes on to ask why it ought, I can give him no other reason than general utility" (2000: 68). Yet doesn't that make every individual's right to security deeply insecure – passing into and out of existence as circumstances change so that the usefulness for society of protecting that person's security changes? If this is true, then his appeal to moral rights will not provide the bright line that Mill seeks for limiting the authority of the state.

Mill needs to show that there is a steady and weighty utility that attaches to the protection of the security of each individual – a utility that remains in place and outweighs local gains in utility that might arise in special circumstances from infringing on an individual's security. Mill seeks to do this in a way that parallels Hume's argument for why it is always advantageous for an individual to comply with the laws of nature. Hume argued that "'tis certain, that the whole plan or scheme is highly conducive, or indeed absolutely requisite, both to the support of society, and the well-being of every individual" and that the whole scheme will collapse if any injustice is done; for "... without justice, society must immediately dissolve, and every one must fall into that savage and solitary condition, which is infinitely worse than the worst situation that can possibly be suppos'd in society" (2000: 319). Mill says that security can be safeguarded only if "the machinery for providing it *is kept unintermittedly in active play*" (2000: 68, emphasis added). *Any* interruption in the protection of security will undercut security at large and, presumably, the resulting loss of utility will be greater than any local gain in utility that might be eked out in special circumstances by infringing on a given individual's utility. Security, Mill says, is "the very groundwork of our existence" (2000: 68).

Mill's slightly earlier essay, *On Liberty* (Mill 1978), famously offers a utilitarian case for unintermitted respect for personal liberty. Mill holds that government is needed "to protect the weaker members of the community from innumerable vultures" (1978: 2). This protection can only be afforded by "an animal of prey stronger than the rest."

> But as the king of the vultures would be no less bent on preying on the flock than any of the minor harpies, it as indispensable to be in a perpetual attitude of defense against his beak and claws. The aim, therefore, of patriots was to set limits to the power which the ruler should be suffered to exercise over the community; and this limitation was what they meant by liberty. (1978: 2)

According to Mill, advocates of democracy came to doubt the need for such limits on the authority of rulers because they held that under democracy the people themselves rule; and the people would never prey upon themselves. However, Mill rejects this line of thought. The operation of democracy has revealed that

> such phrases as "self-government" and "the power of the people over themselves" do not express the true state of the case. The "people" who exercise the power are not always the same people with those over whom it is exercised; and the "self-government" spoken of is not the government of each by himself, but of each by all the rest. (1978: 3–4)

The king of the vultures remains a vulture whose authority must be radically confined. Religious belief has been immunized from political interference by the establishment of "freedom of conscience as an indefeasible right" (1978: 8).

What is needed, though, is a more general principle that broadly confines state authority.[6] To this end, Mill offers a "very simple" libertarian principle.

> That principle is that the sole end for which mankind are warranted, individually or collectively, in interfering with the liberty of action of any of their number is self-protection. That the only purpose for which power can be rightfully exercised over any member of a civilized community, against his will, is to prevent harm to others. (1978: 9)

Mill sums up his presentation of the liberty principle in language one might expect from a natural rights advocate such as Locke. "Over himself, over his own body and mind, the individual is sovereign" (1978: 9).

Nevertheless, Mill quickly adds "It is proper to state that I forego any advantage which could be derived to my argument from the idea of abstract right as a thing independent of utility" (1978: 10). Each individual's claim to freedom rests on the usefulness of that freedom to mankind at large rather than on some bedrock individual right. "Mankind are the greater gainers by suffering each other to live as seems good to themselves than by compelling each to live as seems good to the rest" (1978: 12). Moreover, despite the generality with which the liberty principle is stated, Mill takes the scope of the principle to be more limited than one might at first think.

The principle applies only to thought, expression, and, by extension, to what we might call "lifestyle" choices. According to Mill, what considerations of general utility do underwrite is a strong *presumption* on behalf of freedom of economic action.[7] However, this presumption does not provide an absolute barrier against interference with economic actions. For, each economic action is "a social act" which is therefore subject to social control for the sake of promoting general utility (1978: 94).

Mill offers a variety of arguments on behalf of his principle of personal liberty. We are told that "neither one person, nor any number of persons, is warranted in saying to another human creature of ripe years that he shall not do with his life for his own benefit what he chooses to do with it" (1978: 74). And two considerations support this claim. First, the range of choices under consideration is taken to be limited to choices that do not affect any other party. Second, human creatures of ripe years are more interested in their own well-being and more knowledgeable about what will promote it than society at large. Hence, when society interferes with "purely personal" conduct, "the odds are that it interferes wrongly and in the wrong place" (1978: 81). Unfortunately, the limitation of the liberty principle to *purely* personal conduct leaves a great deal of personal conduct subject to coercive suppression. For

> there are many acts which, being directly injurious only to the agents themselves, ought not to be legally interdicted, but which, if done publically, are a violation of good manners and coming thus within the category of offenses against others, may rightly be prohibited. (1978: 97)

It seems that the sphere of freedom protected by the liberty principle will be vanishingly small unless some independent account of moral rights or justice allows us to distinguish between negative effects on others that are violations of rights or justice and thus qualify for suppression, and negative effects on others that are not violations of rights or justice and thus do not qualify for suppression.

Mill defends freedom of thought, expression, and individual experiments in living on the grounds that these freedoms are necessary for the pursuit and attainment of truth and for autonomous self-development.

> He who lets the world, or his own portion of it, choose his plan of life for him has no need of any other faculty than the ape-like one of imitation. ... But what will be his comparative worth as a human being? It really is of importance, not only what men do, but also what manner of men they are that do it. Among the works of man which human life is rightly employed in perfecting and beautifying, the first in importance surely is man himself. (1978: 56)

Mill's argument here does not seem to be that the pursuit and attainment of truth and autonomous self-development *in turn* lead to happiness. Rather, Mill's claim seems to be that these activities themselves *constitute* the highest form of utility – in contrast to the low utility of lives of ape-like imitation. The danger here is that Mill's argument for liberty for all (civilized) people depends upon a highly specific and contentious view about what type of human life is truly valuable – and what other types should be viewed with contempt.

A different strand of argument in Mill – which reappears in somewhat different guise in Hayek – focuses on the role of free *competition* in thought and expression as a social device for the discovery of truth and the refinement of knowledge by highly fallible beings (1978: 17).

> [T]he peculiar evil of silencing the expression of an opinion is that it is robbing the human race, posterity as well as the existing generation – those who dissent from the opinion, still more than those who hold it. If the opinion is right, they are deprived of the opportunity of exchanging error for truth; if wrong, they lose, what is almost as great a benefit, the clearer perception and livelier impression of truth produced by its collision with error. (1978: 16)

When proceeding entirely on our own in our formation of beliefs we are very likely to go wrong. Our beliefs are certain to be ill-adjusted to reality. Our individual doxastic weakness is remedied by our exposure to truths that other people have managed to attain and also, in a more complex way, by our exposure to falsehoods – the products of the doxastic weaknesses of others – that push us to adjust our own beliefs. There are also cases in which, "the conflicting doctrines, instead of being one true and the other false, share the truth between them, and the nonconforming opinion is needed to supply the remainder of the truth of which the received doctrine embodies only a part" (1978: 44).

We gain from intellectual interaction with others through the exchange of the fruits of our intellectual specialization. Perhaps we gain most when we confront others' aggressive challenges to our respective beliefs. For, even truth-seekers rarely present to themselves the most challenging objections to their own current views.

> Complete liberty of contradicting and disproving our opinion is the very condition which justifies us in assuming its truth for purposes of action; and on no other terms can a being with human faculties have any rational assurance of being right. (1978: 18)

> [B]eing cognizant of all that can, at least obviously, be said against him ... knowing that he has sought for objections and difficulties instead of avoiding them, and shut out no light which can be thrown upon the subject from any quarter – he has a right to think his judgment better than that of any person, or multitude, who have not gone through a similar process. ... The beliefs which we have most warrant for have no safeguard to rest on but a standing invitation to the whole world to prove them unfounded. (1978: 20)

If we describe the goal of participants in this truth-promoting process very abstractly as the advancement of truth, we can say that the coordination among the participants reflects their shared end of advancing truth.[8] However, such a description obscures the competitive nature of the participants' inter- action. Each participant seeks to be the author of the most defensible doctrine within a particular field – where the most defensible doctrine must take account of or rebut other relatively defensible doctrines. To achieve this status, each doctrine must run the gauntlet of the competing views. Out of this discovery process emerges a prized outcome that was not the intended outcome of any one of the parties entering into the process. Truth emerges through an invisible-hand process.

Spencer on the Greatest Happiness Principle and the Law of Equal Freedom

Herbert Spencer was born after Mill, died thirty years after Mill died, and published important works in political theory – especially *The Man versus the State* (1884) and *The Principles of Ethics* (1879–97) decades after Mill's death. Mostly for these reasons, my discussion of Spencer follows that of Mill, even though I will focus on Spencer's early (1851) libertarian work, *Social Statics*. In many ways, *Social Statics* is a deeply problematic work. Spencer's endorsement of the Greatest Happiness Principle is tied to his saying that this principle is the Divine Idea and, in the introduction to this book, Spencer seems to argue that just action, and only just, accords with the Greatest Happiness Principle because God has established justice as the unexceptional path to happiness (1970: 61, 48).[9] More disturbing yet is Spencer's systematic conflation of causal laws of nature – which cannot be violated and must be *relied* upon if happiness is to be attained – and normative principles – which can be violated but must be *abided* by if happiness is to be attained (1970: 37–41). Nevertheless, *Social Statics* is of interest both for Spencer's attempt to base strict regard for his first principle of justice – e.g., the law of equal freedom – on the Greatest Happiness Principle and for the set of moral rights that Spencer derives from that law.

Like Mill's *Utilitarianism* and *On Liberty*, Spencer's *Social Statics* pays tribute to the Greatest Happiness Principle as the ultimate moral standard. Yet, even more so than Mill, Spencer seeks to erect an intermediary principle which, although founded on general utility, provides individuals with principled protection against direct demands upon them in the name of general utility. Spencer draws a sharp line between the acceptance of the greatest happiness as our ultimate moral touchstone and as the end that is to be promoted in all particular actions.

> It is one thing ... to hold that greatest happiness is the creative purpose, and quite a different thing to hold that the greatest happiness should be the immediate aim of man. It has been

the fatal error of the expediency philosophers [in particular, Bentham] to confound these positions. (1970: 61)

The problems with the direct pursuit of the greatest happiness are essentially epistemic. For one thing, there are many competing conceptions of happiness. "[N]o two men have like conceptions; and further, ... in each man the conception is not the same at any two periods of life" (1970: 6). We have no basis for choosing among these conceptions. Moreover, we cannot weigh the attainment of different conceptions against one another. "[I]f we compromise the matter and say [the greatest happiness] should combine both, how much of each shall go to its composition?" (1970: 8). For another thing, even if we had an understanding of the greatest happiness that would allow us to say that one complex social outcome would possess greater happiness than another, we would not know what specific actions would produce that better outcome.

> Granting for the sake of argument that the desideratum, "greatest happiness," is duly comprehended, its identity and nature agreed upon by all, ... there yet remains the unwarranted assumption that it is possible for the self-guided human judgment to determine, with something like precision, by what methods it may be achieved. (1970: 9)

In short, "were the expediency theory otherwise satisfactory, it would still be useless, since it requires nothing less than omniscience to carry it into practice" (1970: 16).

However, Spencer believes that we can discover fundamental principles, compliance with which will lead us in the direction of the greatest happiness – without our having to decide whose conception of happiness is superior. Since each person's chosen exercise of his faculties yields happiness *by that individual's own lights*, the only measure we can have of increases of happiness within society is the percentage of people who are exercising their faculties in accordance with their own choices. The greatest happiness will exist when each member of society is exercising his faculties in accordance with his own choice. So, for Spencer, the greatest happiness requires the advancement of everyone's happiness. The social condition that is crucial to this mutual advancement of happiness is that no one exercises his faculties in ways that block any other person's chosen exercise of her faculties. Thus, the principle most conducive to the greatest happiness is the law of equal freedom, "*Every man has freedom to do all that he wills, provided he infringes not the equal freedom of any other man*" (1970: 95). This law is the fundamental principle of *justice*. Other principles are needed to supplement the law of equal freedom if human beings are to fully attain their potential happiness. For instance, the principle of negative *benevolence* is needed to further limit the exercise of one's faculties to actions that do not cause distress in others. It is a mark of the early stage of human evolution that, even when people comply with the law of equal freedom, their actions often cause distress to others. However, individuals may not be forced not to engage in distressing actions as long as their conduct is respectful of others' equal freedom. In addition, the priority of the law of equal freedom requires us to allow each individual to exercise her freedom in self-harming ways (1970: 69–79).

In *Social Statics*, Spencer proceeds to derive certain more specific rights from the law of equal freedom. I can only discuss a few of the most important or striking such derivations. According to Spencer, the law of equal freedom implies the rights of life and personal liberty. For, if one party kills or enslaves another, the former brings it about that she enjoys a more extensive freedom than the other. Spencer also holds that the law of equal freedom will be violated if one individual possesses discretionary control over the surface of the earth or if a limited number of individuals each possess discretionary control over portions of the total surface of the earth. For, under those circumstances, "the rest of [the earth's] inhabitants can then exercise their faculties – can then exist even – only by consent of the landowners" (1970: 104), whereas the landowners can exercise their faculties without the consent of the landless. Spencer rejects the proposal that equal freedom be preserved by allotting an equal share of the land to each person. For, a scheme of equal division will encounter "the difficulty of fixing the values of respective tracts of land" (1970: 110) and the difficulty of re-fixing values and allotments whenever new individuals come of age (and others die). Instead, Spencer proposes societal ownership of the earth, that is, of all raw materials – although this is to be country-by-country ownership, not global ownership. Such a scheme will realize equal freedom because, "Under it, all men would be equally landlords; all men would be alike free to become tenants" (1970: 110). In *Social Statics*, Spencer advocates what is now known as "left-libertarianism."

According to Spencer, societal ownership of the land also provides the starting point for just individual property rights. For these rights arise from the contracts between society and its tenants. A tenant pays rent to society, and society "to fulfill its part of the agreement, must acknowledge his title to the surplus which remains after the rent has been paid" (1970: 116).[10] Thus, contrary to Locke, Spencer makes the acquisition of all property rights dependent on the consent of society. In contrast, the rights of free speech and the equal rights of women are simple implications of the law of equal freedom. The right to free speech exists, because no individual's speech precludes any other individual's speech (1970: 132). Moreover, "Equity knows no difference of sex. In its vocabulary the word *man* must be understood in the generic and not in the specific sense. The law of equal freedom manifestly applies to the whole race – female as well as male" (1970: 138). Furthermore, Spencer asserts the equal rights of children and, in one of the longest chapters of the book, he contrasts the benefits of non-coercive education with the evils of coercive education (1970: 153–71).

Along with the right *of society* to the earth, the most striking right asserted by Spencer is the right of each individual to ignore the state. Each individual

> is free to drop connection with the state – to relinquish its protection and to refuse to pay toward its support ... in so behaving he in no way trenches upon the liberty of others, for his position is a passive one, and while passive he cannot become an aggressor ... He cannot be coerced into political combination without a breach of the law of equal freedom; he can withdraw from it without committing any such breach, and he has therefore a right so to withdraw. (1970: 185)

Spencer argues that one must endorse this right if one takes at all seriously the common maxim that political authority rests on the consent of the governed. For this must mean the voluntary consent of each person who is to be governed; person C cannot be bound by the consent of A and B. Every act of toleration, for example, of religious dissent, is simply the recognition that in some respect each individual may ignore the state. The right to ignore the state is simply the sum and generalization of such toleration (1970: 191–3). To the dismay of left-libertarians, Spencer removed the chapter on rights to earth from later editions of *Social Statics*; to the dismay of anarchist libertarians, he also removed the chapter on the right to ignore the state.

3
Libertarian Foundations

Introduction

In this chapter and the next I focus on the arguments and insights of the two most well-known, important, and intellectually sophisticated recent defenders of libertarian or libertarian-leaning doctrines, Robert Nozick (1938–2002) and F. A. Hayek (1899–1992). In this chapter, I begin with Nozick's *Anarchy, State, and Utopia* (Nozick 1974) – hereafter, *ASU* – the work that introduced slumbering academic philosophy to political libertarianism. Nozick offers a moral defense of libertarianism based upon his affirmation of Lockean natural rights to life, liberty, and property. I then turn to the quite different sort of argument for individual liberty and liberty-protective principles of justice that Hayek offers in his *The Constitution of Liberty* (Hayek 1960) – hereafter, *CL* – and especially in *Rules and Order* and *The Mirage of Social Justice* (Hayek 1973, 1976) – hereafter *RO* and *MSJ* respectively – which are the first two volumes of his *Law, Legislation, and Liberty*. As we shall see, rather than first defending some fundamental and liberty-friendly moral principle from which further libertarian conclusions are to be derived, Hayek begins by correcting what he takes to be deep errors in our understanding of social order and law. Hayek thinks that crucial mistakes about the character and bases for social order and law have dethroned individual liberty and liberty-protective principles of justice. These values will, however, be reinstated when we understand their essential role in a free, flourishing, and pluralistic social and legal order. In the next chapter, I will turn to the implications concerning the nature of and bases for economic justice and property rights that Nozick and Hayek draw from their foundational claims. (Further groundings for libertarian principles and views about economic justice and property rights are discussed in some detail in this book's bonus online chapter, "Further Philosophical Roads to Libertarianism.")

Nozick on the Separateness of Persons, Moral Side Constraints, and Rights

Any discussion of Nozick's views must begin with his bold opening claim from the Preface of *ASU*: "Individuals have rights, and there are things no person or group may do to them (without violating their rights)" (1974: ix). Toward the end of that Preface, Nozick also states that *ASU* does not provide "a precise theory of the moral basis of individual rights" (1974: xiv). However, this admission does not justify the contention of many critics that Nozick provides no underpinning for individual moral rights.[1] I will present a sympathetic reconstruction of Nozick's admittedly sketchy case for affirming certain individual rights.[2] John Rawls' *A Theory of Justice* (Rawls 1971) – hereafter, *TJ* – stands as the late twentieth century's blockbuster in political philosophy – especially in light of the way in which this work paved the way for Rawls' somewhat revised account of the principles of justice in *Political Liberalism* (Rawls 1993) hereafter *PL*. I will argue that Nozick provides at least as much argumentation for his affirmation of moral rights as John Rawls provides for the contractarian project that he develops in *TJ*. Indeed, Nozick's argument for the affirmation of individual rights essentially replicates Rawls' argument for the contractarian program of identifying the principles of justice by ascertaining what principles rational individuals would agree upon to govern their interactions (or to govern the design of the basic institutions that will govern their interactions). I shall further contend that this common argument *better* justifies Nozick's affirmation of individual rights than Rawls' contractarian project.

In *TJ*, Rawls sets out to oust utilitarianism as the dominant doctrine in political philosophy and replace it with his particular version of contractarianism. Rawls' strategy is to identify what he takes to be the signature argument on behalf of utilitarianism, debunk that argument, and display his contractarian approach as the alternative that most or most obviously avoids the error detected within that argument for utilitarianism (1971: 22–33). The core contention that Rawls ascribes to utilitarianism is that, if a certain principle of individual choice is sound, then so too is a certain principle of social choice. The principle of *individual* choice is that, at least if no other party is affected, it is rational for an individual to incur costs for himself (or to forego benefits for himself) if doing so will spare him greater costs (or provide him with greater benefits) – if by doing so he will "achieve his own greatest good" (1971: 23). The principle of *social* choice is that it is rational for each member of society to engender costs or forego benefits for *any* member of society if doing so will spare *any* other member (or group of members) of society greater costs, or provide that other member (or group of members) with greater benefits. According to Rawls, the utilitarian holds that the maximizing rationale that supports the principle of individual choice likewise supports the principle of social choice. Thus, according to the utilitarian, each agent as a member of society has reason to maximize the aggregate social good even at the expense of the individual good of himself or others. "The principle of choice for an association of men is interpreted as an extension of the principle of choice for one man" (1971: 24).

Rawls rejects this transition from this principle of individual choice to this principle of social choice. He maintains that this transition fails to recognize the fundamental difference between individuals and society. That difference is that persons are markedly more separate and distinct from one another than are the different phases of a given person's life from one another. Those different phases are all parts of a single individual life, while individual lives are not anything like all parts of a single social life. A greater gain in one phase of an individual's life and a lesser loss in another phase will be a greater gain and a lesser loss *for that individual*. There is some entity, viz., that individual, for whom that gain at the expense of that loss will be *worthwhile*. Because of this, that individual will have reason to incur that loss in order to capture that gain. In contrast, the lives of individuals do not add up to a social life for which – from the perspective of which – it is worthwhile that a loss be incurred in one of those individual lives if that loss engenders a greater gain in another one of those individual lives. There is no subject who undergoes both the greater gain and the lesser loss such that we can say that this subject is compensated for the lesser loss by the greater gain. The fundamental error of utilitarianism is that it "does not take seriously the distinction between persons" (1971: 27).

Of course, a particular member of society might gain by way of another member incurring a loss. That individual may have reason to be pleased about her benefiting at the expense of the other. Nevertheless, the question is whether that gain provides a reason for the party who will undergo the loss to incur that loss (or to accept its imposition upon her) in anything like the way there would be reason for her to undergo it were she also to reap the greater gain. Rawls answers this question in the negative. According to Rawls, only if we conflate individuals – only if we mistakenly conceive of them as parts of a single person-like being, will the utilitarian principle of social choice be on a par with the principle of individual choice (1971: 26–7). However, society is not such a fusion of individuals. Society is an association of individuals; it is not itself an entity with a life of its own. Rawls concludes that,

> if we assume that the correct regulative principle for anything depends on the nature of that thing, and the plurality of distinct persons with separate systems of ends is an essential feature of human societies, we should not expect the principles of social choice to be utilitarian. (1971: 29)

Notice that Rawls takes his critique to carry him beyond the mere dismissal of the utilitarian regulative principle. For, he takes that critique to reveal a criterion for the correct regulative principle (or set of principles) for the governance of social interaction. Correct regulative principles must be responsive to or reflective of "the plurality of distinct persons with separate systems of ends." For this reason, we should expect the correct regulative principles to be fundamentally different in character from the utilitarian principle of social choice. For Rawls, the mark of such principles is that they would be agreed to by all members of society were they all to bargain rationally with one another about what principles will govern their interaction. If certain principles would be agreed to by all rational individuals – each of whom is interested in advancing her distinct system of ends[3] – those principles can be said to take seriously the separateness of persons. The core of the argument for the superiority of Nozick's natural rights reading of the implications of the separateness argument is that Rawls' contractarian reading of the argument's implications more betrays than recognizes "the plurality of distinct persons with separate systems of ends."

Nozick's version of the separateness argument also begins with his wondering whether we should proceed from the principle of individual choice to the utilitarian principle of social choice.

> Individually, we each sometimes choose to undergo some pain or sacrifice for a greater benefit or to avoid a greater harm: we go to the dentist to avoid worse suffering later ... In each case, some cost is borne for the sake of the greater overall good. Why not, similarly, hold that some persons have to bear some costs that benefit other persons more, for the sake of the overall social good? (1974: 32)

Nozick's response to this question is,

> But there is no *social entity* with a good that undergoes some sacrifice for its own good. There are only individual people, different individual people, with their own individual lives. Using one of these people for the benefit of others, uses him and benefits the others. Nothing more. What happens is that something is done to him for the sake of others. Talk of an overall social good covers this up. (1974: 32–3)

Nevertheless, it may be unfair to the utilitarian to hold that her argument depends on the fusing or conflation of persons or belief in a social entity. A forthright utilitarian may be quite willing to say that greater gains bestowed on one individual justify the lesser losses imposed on some separate individual. Let us consider one elegant way for a utilitarian to attempt to uphold the inference from the principle of individual choice to the utilitarian principle of social choice without relying on the conflation of persons into a social entity.

This utilitarian would claim that what makes it rational for an individual to incur a lesser cost within her own life in order to attain a greater benefit within her own life is simply that *the benefit is greater than the cost*. The fact that the cost and the benefit are *hers* – that they both occur with her life – plays no role in making rational the production of the greater benefit at the lesser cost. Therefore, no contentious inference is needed to get from the *so-called* principle of individual choice to the principle of social choice. For, what is already really at work in making the personally advantageous action rational is simply the impersonal principle that it is rational to incur costs (on whomever they will fall) whenever doing so will yield more extensive gains (on whomever they are bestowed). Rawls and Nozick depict the utilitarian as trying to assimilate the utilitarian principle of social choice to the principle of individual choice by thinking of society as a mega-individual. "[U]tilitarianism is not individualistic, at least as arrived at by the more natural course of reflection, in that, by conflating all systems of desires, it applies to society the principle of choice for one man" (1971: 29). In contrast, this alternative utilitarian strategy seeks to assimilate the principle of (apparent) individual choice to the utilitarian principle of social choice by stripping the principle of individual choice of its individualism. If one accepts the latter assimilation, one can move with remarkable ease from the de-personalized principle of (apparent) individual choice to the explicitly impersonal utilitarian principle of social choice.

To counter this alternative utilitarian strategy, Rawls and Nozick need to hold that what makes it rational for a given individual to incur some cost *to herself* (or forego some benefit *for herself*) is the avoidance of some greater cost *to herself* (or the attainment of some greater benefit *for herself*). They must hold that the utilitarian principle of social choice is not already embedded in what (therefore) only appears to be a distinct principle of individual choice. They need to maintain that the rationality of prudential behavior, that is, incurring lesser costs *within one's own life* for the sake of greater gains *within one's own life*, is distinct from and far less contentious than the rationality of engendering lesser costs whenever doing so will realize greater gains without regard to who will bear the costs and who will reap the gains. Then they can say that the real task for the utilitarian is to transition from the rationality of prudence to the distinct and at least apparently much more contentious utilitarian principle of social choice. And they can go on to say that it is hard to imagine anyone attempting to make this arduous transition without thinking that society is itself a type of mega-individual composed of conflated individuals.

And, certainly, Rawls' statement of the principle of individual choice presents it as a distinct (and prudential[4]) principle. "A person *quite properly* acts, at least when others are not affected, to achieve *his own greatest good*, to advance *his rational ends* as far as possible." And "the principle for an individual is to advance as far as possible *his own* welfare, *his own* system of desires" (1971: 23, emphasis added). There is no hint within this statement of the principle of individual choice that the ends of others are among – indeed, are *equally* among – one's own rational ends. The same note is struck when Nozick expresses his complaint against the utilitarian argument by saying of each individual whose loss is taken to provide a greater gain to others, "He does not get some overbalancing good from his sacrifice". Similarly, Nozick parses "the fact of our separate existences" as

> the fact that no moral balancing act can take place among us; there is no moral outweighing of one of our lives by others so as to lead to a great overall social good. There is no justified sacrifice of some of us for others. (1974: 33)

Costs and benefits can be balanced against one another *within* persons' lives but not *across* them. This is the message of the principle of individual choice. This is why the utilitarian principle of social choice is not implicitly embedded within it, and this is why one should expect at least considerable difficulty in transitioning from the principle of individual choice to the utilitarian principle of social choice.

Like Rawls, Nozick thinks that a further lesson is to be drawn from the separateness argument. The argument does not merely allow one to reject a proposed justification for imposing sacrifices on some to benefit others. It also leads us, in Rawls' words, to affirm for each member of society "an inviolability founded on justice or, as some say, on natural right, which even the welfare of society as a whole cannot override" (1971: 28). We need to see what further lesson Nozick draws from the shared separateness argument, how Nozick draws that lesson, and why the lesson drawn by Nozick is more true to the separateness argument than is the lesson that Rawls draws.

Nozick takes "the fact of our separate existences" to entail that "no moral balancing act can take place among us." This rejection of moral balancing undermines the utilitarian's attempt at a positive justification for the imposition of sacrifices. However, the rejection of moral balancing does not as such establish the wrongfulness of such impositions. How then can Nozick get to the *further* claim that imposing sacrifices on people *wrongs* them? He seeks to do this by appealing to the idea that each person's actions must "*sufficiently respect and take account of* the fact that [each other individual] is a separate person, and his is the only life he has" (1974: 33, emphasis added). Inflicting sacrifices on Ben fails to sufficiently respect and take account of the fact of Ben's separate existence as a being who rationally pursues his own system of ends. The requirement that, in one's conduct toward others, one sufficiently respect and take account of their existence as separate, purposive beings with ends of their own mandates circumspection in one's treatment of them. It mandates moral side constraints on one's conduct toward others. As Nozick puts it, "The moral side constraints upon what we may do, I claim, *reflect* the fact of our separate existences. They *reflect* the fact that no moral balancing act can take place among us" (1974: 33, emphasis added).

It is no coincidence that these claims on Nozick's part are reminiscent of Locke's arguments for natural moral rights in §6 of the *Second Treatise*. Each of us has a life of our own within which each of us seeks to advance our personal good. What is the import for each individual of this fact about all other individuals? What is the response on the part of each individual that indicates taking seriously "the existence of distinct individuals" understood in this way? The response cannot be a utilitarian disposition to impose sacrifices on some for the greater good of others – as though individuals exist for one another's purposes. Rather, the import is a restriction on the ways in which each individual may seek to advance her ends, viz., a restriction against advancing her ends in ways that treat others as though they exist for her purposes. The existence of distinct individuals "underlies the existence of moral side constraints" because to take seriously the separateness of persons is to take seriously the fact that distinct individuals, as Locke says, are not "made for one another's uses" (1980: §6) and as Nozick says, are "not resources for others" (1974: 33). Recall that Rawls says, "A person quite properly acts, *at least when others are not affected*, to achieve his own greatest good, to advance his rational ends as far as possible" (1971: 23, emphasis added). What about when others are or can be affected? The utilitarian answer is that, when others are or can be affected, one must give up the (otherwise proper) goal of achieving one's own good and, instead, devote oneself to the advancement of the aggregate good. Nozick's answer is that, when others are or can be affected, one must be circumspect in one's conduct so as to avoid treating others – who each "quite properly" seek their own good – as though they are resources at one's own disposal.

These contentions invite expression in the Kantian language of persons being ends in themselves and, therefore, not being means – or mere means – for the ends of others. According to Nozick, since each individual is an end-in-himself in the sense of having a life of his own within which he rationally seeks to advance his own system of desires or interests, each is not to be treated as a means to the ends of others; no one is to be treated as a resource at the disposal of other people. We *honor* others as agents with rational ends of their own not by promoting their ends as we do our own – to follow that course would be to treat ourselves as means to others' ends – but, rather, by not sacrificing others to our ends. On this construal, the kingdom of ends is the social order in which each individual has sovereign authority over herself and recognizes each other individual's like moral sovereignty

Nozick is concerned that his unqualified condemnation of using others as means will support anti-libertarian prohibitions, for example, prohibitions against taking pleasure in another person's appearance or trading with another person to one's advantage. He then rules out such implications by declaring that, for the purposes of political philosophy, we need only be concerned "with *certain* ways that persons may not use others: primarily, physically aggressing against them" (1974: 33). However, this restriction is *ad hoc* because no reason is given for why political philosophy should only be concerned with this subset of usings. If all usings of another are comparably problematic as failures to take seriously the separate existence of their subjects, then all such usings should equally be the concern of political philosophy. Nozick would have done better to explain why only certain usings of others especially offend against the fact that other individuals have systems of ends of their own to pursue, lives of their own to live. He might have argued that the usings of others that especially offend against the import of others having ends of their own to promote are those that interfere with others' pursuits of their own good. Non-interfering "uses" – such as taking pleasure in another's appearance or trading with a (consenting) other person to one's advantage – are not usings in the sense that would bring them within the ambit of political philosophy.

On Nozick's view, Jen is subject to certain moral side constraints in her conduct toward Ben because of Ben's *standing* as a separate purposive being with rational ends of his own, with a life of his own to live. Ben's correlative rights against Jen not to be treated as though he exists as a resource to serve her ends is likewise a matter of Ben's moral standing. When Ben asserts these rights, he is asserting this moral *status*, and when Jen acknowledges those rights, she is acknowledging that status. It is this status that Jen honors when she is appropriately circumspect in her conduct toward Ben. This status provides Jen with a reason to be circumspect in her comportment toward Ben that is not based on the *value* for Jen, for Ben, or for society of her circumspection.

Jen may well have *value-based* reasons to be circumspect in her conduct toward Ben. For example, it may well be that attacking Ben for the purpose of enslaving him will be detrimental to Jen's own rational ends – because Ben will fight back or because Jen would do better by establishing long-term cooperative interaction with Ben. However, such negative consequences for Jen of attacking Ben do not account for Ben having a *right* against Jen that she not attack him. Suppose that, faced with the prospect of Jen's attack, Ben asserts his right not to be attacked and in response Jen says, "You are right; my attacking you would have bad consequences for me." Ben will quite properly say, "Jen, you missed the point of my asserting a right not to be attacked. You mistakenly think that my right against the attack depends on the negative consequences (for you) of engaging in the attack. But my right does not flow from and is not hostage to those negative consequences." As Locke points out, a farmer may have good value-based reasons not to destroy a useful cow just as a Hobbesian sovereign may have good value-based reasons not to destroy a useful subject; but in neither case is the master recognizing a *right* of the subject not to be destroyed (1980: §93).

Similarly, Ben may well have *value-based* reasons to oppose being attacked by Jen. However, in asserting his right not to be attacked, he is not merely pointing to the bad consequences for him (or for others) of his being subject to the attack. It is Ben's moral status, not the fact that this attack would be contrary to certain of his interests, which undergirds his *right* against being attacked by Jen. In short, the moral impermissibility of Jen attacking Ben is not dependent on the disvalue of that attack for Jen or Ben or (even) for society at large. This is why we can condemn any such attack without first engaging in an often complex empirical investigation about the consequences of the attack for Jen or Ben or (even) for society at large. More generally, the ascription of basic rights to people not to be treated as though they are resources who may be disposed of to advance the goals of others (or even their own goals) allows us to condemn unprovoked killing, or enslaving, or maiming of any individual without first having to engage in an often uncertain and indecisive "calculus of social interests" [Rawls 1971: 4]. All this brings out the anti-consequentialist character of Nozick's doctrine of rights. According to consequentialist doctrines, the end always ultimately justifies the means. The Nozickean anti-consequentialist stance is that there are reasons to eschew certain means of promoting one's goals – reasons that arise from the character of those modes of conduct and not from the disvalue of the consequences of that conduct. (Recall here the prominence of *constraining principles* in the thought of Locke and Hume and the felt need of consequentialists like Mill and Spencer to extract such principles from considerations of utility.)

It is common for consequentialists to maintain that it would be bizarre for there to be sound moral norms that were utterly detached from the value of what those norms protect. This is correct. However, on Nozick's view, the case for moral side constraints that protect individuals from interference with their (non-interfering) promotion of their own ends is hardly utterly detached from the value of persons fulfilling their own system of desires or interests. For compliance with that protective moral side constraint is required in order to sufficiently respect and take account of – to honor – the value that such fulfillment has for each individual who attains it. However, since the value of others' fulfillment of their respective rational ends need not be value that one must oneself promote, that fulfillment need not be a goal for one's own actions. The deep feature of libertarian thinking is that the value of each person's happiness or well-being does not mean that everyone has enforceable obligations to promote everyone's happiness or well-being.

That each individual is a separate and independent being with ends of her own provides each of us with reason to affirm each individual's moral rights against being subject to (unprovoked) killing, assault, maiming, or enslaving. The fact that Nozick's separateness argument provides a unifying explanation for our strong pre-theoretical judgments that there are rights against such forms of treatment further validates that argument. Only a bit later in *ASU* does Nozick appeal to the idea of "moral space" and an understanding of moral rights as defining the boundaries of each individual's moral space. "A line (or hyper-plane) circumscribes an area in moral space around an individual. Locke holds that this line is determined by an individual's natural rights, which limit the action of others" (1974: 57). Due to this division of moral space into "mine" and "thine," "[i]ndividual rights are co-possible; each person may exercise his rights as he chooses" (1974: 106) without interfering with any other individual's exercise of her rights.

Consider why any proposed rights need to form a co-possible set of rights. A set of rights is supposed to specify what the right-holders must be allowed to do. However, if those rights are not co-possible, a particular action by one person may be both an exercise of her rights and an infringement on some other person's rights. In such a case, whether the act is to be allowed or disallowed will depend upon there being a plausible doctrine that indicates which right it is better to protect. And, either there will be no such doctrine – because "no moral balancing act can take place among us" (1974: 33) – in which case the proposed set of rights will not specify what right-holders must be allowed to do. Or, there will be a doctrine that indicates which right it is better to protect. In that case, that doctrine, rather than the set of proposed rights, will determine what people must be allowed to do.

The need for the basic ascription of rights to be co-possible,[5] combined with the naturalness of thinking of rights as defining a moral sphere (or domain) within which the right-holder may do as she sees fit and the boundaries of which may not crossed by others without the right-holder's permission, leads naturally to thinking of basic rights as a type of property or ownership – or a type of jurisdiction over the objects of one's rights.

> The central core of the notion of a property right in X, relative to which other parts of the notion are to be explained, is the right to determine what shall be done with X; the right to choose which of the constrained set of options concerning X shall be realized or attempted ... My property rights in my knife allow me to leave it where I will, but not in your chest. I may choose which of the acceptable options involving the knife is to be realized. This notion of property helps us understand why earlier theorists spoke of people as having property in themselves and their labor. They viewed each person as having a right to decide what would become of himself and

what he would do, and as having a right to reap the benefits
of what he did. (1974: 171)

The most auspicious way of thinking about co-possible rights
that will provide moral protection for each person is to think
of those rights as property rights, as forms of ownership.
And the most salient thing that each individual must have
ownership over, if rights are to protect each individual in
her pursuit of her own ends in constraint-compliant ways,
is *her own person*. The first component of the moral space
or domain that it makes sense to ascribe to each individual
is *herself*, that is, her own physical and mental resources and
powers.

I've said that Nozick deviates from Rawls in the lesson
that he draws from the separateness argument. Rawls takes
the lesson to be that these principles must be the ones that
rational individuals would agree upon were they to bargain
(in appropriate circumstances) about what principles would
govern their association. Thus, for Rawls, we cannot know
what principles govern our interactions until we figure out
what principles (if any) all rational individuals would agree
to within the circumstances that we identify as appropriate
for such agreement.[6] In contrast, Nozick does not think that
we have to figure out how to characterize the contractarian
"original position," the level of knowledge and the type
of motivations that individuals should be thought to have
within that position, and what principles those individuals
would all agree to in that position in order to ascertain, at
least in broad terms, what principles of justice or natural
rights are reflective of the separateness of persons.

Taking seriously the separateness of others requires that
we not treat others as means to our own ends, that we
not impose losses on them to advance our own purposes.
Further articulation of this basic natural moral constraint
on our conduct supports each individual's basic natural
right to do as she sees fit with her own person (but not, of
course, with other persons). And this basic right encom-
passes natural rights against being subjected to unprovoked
killing, assault, enslavement, and maiming. Moreover, such
treatment violates one's rights *whatever* the specific purpose
of the party who inflicts that treatment. Nozick takes the

separateness argument to delegitimize any conception of an overall social good that calls upon individuals to sacrifice and to impose sacrifices for its advancement. Imposing a loss on one individual for the sake of enhancing equality among the members of society or for the sake of enhancing the well-being of the least well-off members of society is as much precluded as imposing losses on that individual for the sake of increasing aggregate utility.

What is wrong with utilitarianism is not limited to the particular social outcome that it enshrines but extends to its more general, consequentialist supposition that, whatever the favored social end is, no one can have a right against what needs to be done to promote that end. Rawls tells us that if "the plurality of distinct persons with separate systems of ends is an essential feature of human societies, we should not expect the principles of social choice to be utilitarian" (1971: 29). However, the appropriate and more general conclusion is that we should not expect the principles that govern inter-actions among individuals to specify any common end or hierarchy of ends, the promotion of which is taken to justify the imposition of sacrifices upon individuals.[7] If the nature of society is that it is an association of distinct persons who quite properly seek to promote their discrete systems of ends, we should expect that the basic regulative principles for society are – as Hayek says – end-independent principles. That is, they are principles that do not enshrine any common, substantive end or system of ends but, rather, protect or facilitate each individual's pursuit of her own separate and distinct system of ends. We should not expect principles, like those advocated by Rawls – that is, principles that specify how various primary goods are to be distributed among the members of society, and that rank alternative institutional structures on the basis of how extensively they realize those distributions – to be the correct regulative principles.

I want to complete the argument for the *greater plausibility* of the lesson drawn by Nozick by noting a couple of ways in which the contractarian project that Rawls takes to be underwritten by the separateness argument fails to "take seriously the plurality and distinctness of individuals" (1971: 29). First, the contractarian project makes whatever basic *rights* an individual has conceptually dependent upon it being worthwhile to others to accord this individual those rights; for it is that value to others of ascribing rights to that individual that provides others with reason to agree to them. Within the original position, individuals do not have moral standing on their own – albeit each has the moral power to withhold moral standing from others. The second and more commonly noted way in which Rawls' contractarian project does not take seriously the separateness of persons is that in Rawls' original position no individual is allowed to have any knowledge about who in particular she (or anyone else) is. There is no distinctness of systems of ends and no distinctness of persons. This enables Rawls to say that all he needs to figure out is what any one of these *depersonalized* individuals would most favor in the way of regulative principles in order to ascertain what they all would agree to. For, every equally *depersonalized* individual in the original position will necessarily most favor and agree to the same principles. Somewhere between Rawls' deployment of the separateness argument and his adoption and development of the contractarian project, separate and distinct persons with moral standing of their own slip through the cracks.

Hayek on Social Order, Freedom, and the Rules of Just Conduct

Unlike the other theorists who are discussed in this and subsequent chapters who were trained as and earned their livelihoods as academic philosophers, F.A. Hayek was trained as an academic economist[8] and the primary focus of his work from the early 1930s through the mid-1940s was in economic theory. For this work he was a co-recipient of the Nobel Prize in Economics in 1974. In the early 1940s, Hayek's attention shifted to political and legal theory. Hayek published an enormous number of important essays and books in these areas from his 1944 *The Road to Serfdom* to his 1988 *The Fatal Conceit*. His two outstanding works of political and legal philosophy within this period are *The Constitution of Liberty* and the three-volume work

Law, Legislation, and Liberty. Both these treatises seek to provide a restatement of strongly classical liberal principles – although the policy recommendations that accompany these restatements are often less libertarian than one would expect. Hayek's recurrent insistence on the importance of strict loyalty to certain liberty-friendly principles is often accompanied by the endorsement of certain coercive state actions that seem to contravene those principles.

It is a bit unclear what Hayek has in mind when offering a "restatement" of fundamental principles. Hayek's restatements seem to be offered as justifications; yet the use of "restatements" seems to be Hayek's way of tiptoeing between his desire to offer justifications for liberty-friendly principles and his sense that to offer such vindications is to engage in illicit inferences from "claims capable of a scientific resolution" to "judgments of value" (1973: 6). Hayek may think that he can avoid reliance upon such an inference because of the way in which different claims about the nature of social order and law – claims that *are* capable of scientific assessment – give rise to different judgments of value. As he sees it, mistaken views about the nature of social order and law give rise to certain judgments of value that are unsound, at least in the sense that they presuppose those mistaken factual views. These unsound judgments of value "dethrone" the judgments of value that would reign were scientifically correct understandings of the nature of social order in place. Correlatively, the reinstatement of a correct understanding of social order and law will re-enthrone judgments of value that are sound in the sense that the acceptance of these values is essential to the existence of a social and legal order that fosters robust cooperation to mutual advantage.

Thus, according to Hayek, the real action lies within disputes about the nature of and conditions for social order and law; and his socialist opponents are not to be attacked for their wicked values but, rather, for their mistaken social scientific doctrines. Statist doctrines

> are false, not because of the values on which they are based, but because of a misconception of the forces which have made the Great Society and civilization possible. The demonstration that the differences between socialists and non-socialists

ultimately rest on purely intellectual issues capable of a scientific resolution and not on different judgments of value appears to me one of the most important outcomes of the train of thought in this book ... [The] destruction of values by scientific error ... has increasingly come to seem to me the great tragedy of our time – a tragedy, because the values which scientific error tends to dethrone are the indispensable foundation of all our civilization. (1973: 6–7)

Following Hayek's lead, I will focus first and primarily on his contrast between different conceptions of social order and law. This, indeed, is probably his most important contribution to classical liberal and libertarian thought. I will begin with a crucial early moment in Hayek's intellectual career and present further developments in Hayek's thought as a deepening and generalization of the insights about social order and law from that crucial early moment.[9] Hayek offers an essentially Millian restatement of the case for liberty in *The Constitution of Liberty* and an essentially Humean restatement of the case for liberty-protective principles of justice in *Law, Legislation, and Liberty*.[10] I shall focus on the latter, more successful restatement.

Like Nozick (Raico 2002), in his student days, Hayek thought of himself as a democratic socialist. Shortly thereafter, Hayek's reading of Ludwig von Mises' *Socialism* [Mises 1981] persuaded him of the defects of socialism and the virtues of an economic order based on private ownership and market relationships.[11] Speaking of himself as one of the many "young idealists returning to their university studies [in Vienna] after World War I," Hayek wrote, "Socialism promised to fulfill our hopes for a more rational, more just world. And then came this book. Our hopes were dashed. *Socialism* told us that we had been looking for improvement in the wrong direction" (1981: xix). One of the most powerful attractions of socialism throughout the nineteenth century and well into the twentieth was the idea that rational economic order had to be planned order. According to this idea, the creation of an economic order should be thought of as an engineering project. Just as the rational creation of a bridge requires a careful inventory of the material and human resources that are available for the bridge's construction, a determination of precisely what role each of these resources will best serve in that construction, and the issuance of detailed directives to the human resources at hand,[12] the rational creation of an economic order requires a like process of inventory, design, and direction (1964: 94–102). In order to have a rational economic system, all economic activity has to be organized through a single, comprehensive plan for the utilization of all of society's economic resources so as to best achieve society's goals.

Mises' elegant argument against central economic planning turns on its inability to allocate economic resources rationally. The rational allocation of economic resources is essentially a matter of devoting low-value inputs to the production of high-value outputs; it is a matter of maximizing the difference between the value of the basic inputs of production and the value of the final consumer products. Thus, rational allocation depends upon *knowledge* of the value of the many different sorts of inputs, the value of all the different sorts of the intermediary products – e.g., enhanced labor and capital goods – that more basic inputs might be used to produce, and the value of the many sorts of final consumer products that might be produced by the many different possible allocations of basic and enhanced inputs. Mises' revolutionary insight is that knowledge of the relevant economic values is available only in the form of market prices. For the value of this or that input or output is a function of the relative scarcity of and demand for those specific inputs and outputs; and market prices are formed by and encapsulate the best information that individuals possess about the current (and future) relative scarcity of and demand for this or that input or output. However, central economic planning eliminates markets and, hence, market prices. Thus, central economic planning eliminates the possibility of the information that central economic planning needs in order to achieve the rational allocation of economic resources.

To make Mises' point more intuitively vivid, imagine that you are assigned the job of central planner for the economy of some society. And let us make the *totally unrealistic* supposition that you are presented with a comprehensive list of all the material and human resources available for your plan and of the results of an exhaustive study of what products people have *said* they would like to have. So, you would have information about where under the ground certain mineral deposits lay and where certain machinery was that might be used to mine this or that mineral (but also might be used to dig canals or contour golf courses) and what sorts of delivery systems exist for moving machinery or ore to factories or manufactured consumer products to local distribution centers. Now you have to decide how many washing machines and of which size and what quality should be manufactured and out of which material, for example stainless steel or aluminum or titanium. Of course, you also have to decide how much stainless steel or aluminum or titanium should be devoted to producing buses, air conditioners, surgical implants, and statues of the Great Leader.

How could you rationally make any of these decisions in the absence of knowledge of the value of all the inputs and outputs at issue? And how could you have knowledge of those values in the absence of market prices? What would people be willing to pay – *if they had money to pay with* – to purchase tickets to see the Great Leader's statue? How much more or less would that be than people would be willing to pay – *if they had money to pay with* – for each of the other uses of the resources that would go into the production of that statue? Consider why *we* all know that it would be insane for a central planner to order that washing machines be made out of titanium rather than stainless steel. The reason is that, while most of us know very little about the extent of the supply of and many alternative uses for titanium and stainless steel, we all know that the *price* per unit of titanium is vastly greater than that of stainless steel.[13]

Hayek further develops this Misesian argument, in a series of articles in the 1930s on the "Socialist Calculation" debate,[14] by emphasizing an additional category of information that central planners would not possess. This is information that would not be reflected in – or would barely be reflected in – market prices even were market prices not eliminated by central planning. This information is the highly particular knowledge – or hunches – that individual economic agents have about local circumstances, for example, knowledge about an unused piece of machinery that could be brought back into service, or about a local artisan's as yet unrecognized ability to modify that piece of machinery, or about the suitability of one raw material as a substitute for the commonly used material in some productive process, or about the degree of demand that will exist for an as-yet non-existent good or service.

Often this highly dispersed information is tacit; individuals have the information in the sense that it is available to guide their actions even though they have not made it explicit to themselves. Individuals often only tacitly know that they can carry out some particular task or how they would weigh against one another the fulfillment of their various goals. Often the dispersed information will be in the form of "know-how" rather than in the form of known propositions. On Hayek's view, successful economic action – especially successful economic *innovation* – is deeply dependent upon decisions that draw upon such radically dispersed information. This information is even more inaccessible to central planners than the information that would be conveyed by market prices.

We should note that the Misesian–Hayekian argument provides the third of three types of criticisms of socialism, none of which appeal directly to high moral principles. The first is the interest critique. Socialism provides too little incentive to individuals for productive activity and too much incentive for slacking off. The second is the power critique. Socialist regimes dangerously centralize and expand state power which is likely to be captured by the most politically ambitious and ruthless people. The third is the knowledge critique. Socialist planning requires more knowledge than the planners could possibly have. To be clear, the knowledge that planners will lack is knowledge of factual particulars, for example, knowledge of the existence of this or that particular material resource or some unrecognized consumer preference. The mind of the central planner lacks a synoptic grasp of such factual matters. This ignorance of current facts radically undercuts the central planner's capacity to predict the particular future effects of current actions.

It is one thing to show that central planning will not yield a rational allocation of economic resources and another thing to show that an economic regime centering on private property and market interactions will yield such an allocation.[15] Still, the rational allocation case for private property/free market regimes is pretty much the mirror image of the Misesian–Hayekian case against central planning. The crucial move is the recognition that decentralizing (i.e., de-politicizing) economic decision-making brings dispersed, local information into play. Private holders of economic resources – raw materials, special skills and know-how, information, and capital goods – seek to reap the greatest return from these resources. They do so by themselves employing those resources in the ways that they perceive will maximize their respective returns – including their rental or sale of their resources to yet other agents who perceive high-return uses for those resources. Guided by prices and alert to changes in them, owners of economic resources seeking higher returns discover or create opportunities to move relatively lower valued resources to higher valued uses. Individuals with information about their own prospects as bakers – including a sense of their own talents and of what standard or yet to be introduced baked goods brewers and butchers will value – turn to baking; and likewise for potential brewers and butchers.

The adjustments of individuals who are free to choose how and in coordination with whom they will employ their own resources will be systemically more rational in terms of efficient allocation than those that would be ordered by any central planner because they are guided both by the price information generated by markets and the local information those individuals will have.[16]

> In civilized society it is indeed not so much the greater knowledge that the individual can acquire, as the greater benefit he receives from the knowledge possessed by others, which is the cause of his ability to pursue an infinitely wider range of ends than merely the satisfaction of his most pressing physical needs. (1973: 14)

The results of these adjustments are typically remarkably complex and complexly interrelated chains of cooperative interaction involving people who are barely known or are utterly unknown to one another and which as a whole are unplanned. As Hayek puts it in his highly influential 1944 essay, "The Use of Knowledge in Society,"

> The whole acts as one market, not because any of its members survey the whole field, but because their limited individual fields of vision sufficiently overlap so that through many intermediaries the relevant information is communicated to all. (1948 [1945]: 86)

Adam Smith pointed out that no one plans the enormously complex network of cooperative interactions that leads from the miner who mines the ore that becomes the shepherd's shears to the shepherd to the wool cloth manufacturer to the urban worker's wool coat (1981: 22–3). Nor does anyone plan the network of production, exchange, and distribution that brings every sort of footwear that anyone in your city might want to wear to some outlet in (or virtually in) your city. Such chains of coordination arise through a multitude of *individually planned* actions; but the chains as a whole and the larger yet networks of such chains are not intended by, and could not be successfully planned by, anyone.

This is not *at all* to say that people are moved only by the prospect of economic gain. Indeed, it is not *at all* to say that pecuniary gain is among *anyone's* ultimate ends. "There are, in the last resort, no economic ends" (Hayek 1976: 113). Furthermore, the benefits that arise among people when they are free to seek cooperative solutions to their problems on the basis of their own understanding of their circumstances and purposes are hardly limited to pecuniary gains. As imperfect as people's choices are about who they will marry or how they will arrange their family vacations or what sort of religious affiliation (if any) they will enter into, people are at least very likely to do better being free to make these arrangements on their own than by obeying the commands of the central planning boards for marriage, vacations, and religious affiliation.

For Hayek, what emerges from the Socialist Calculation debate is an understanding that there are two alternative conceptions of *social order* and, correspondingly, two alternative conceptions of *law* that make order possible. There is designed, *top-down* order, in which the particular elements within that order are arranged in accordance with an organizer's plan and *top-down* law that consists of directives issued by the organizer. In contrast, there is spontaneous order

– *ground-up* order that emerges through the interaction and mutual adjustment of the elements that make up the resulting order and *ground-up* law that consists of evolved constraints on conduct that protect individuals in their chosen actions and mutual adjustments.

As an example of a designed social order, consider an army engaged in a large-scale military campaign. The central command surveys all the human and material resources at its disposal and all the (salient) combinations of ways that those resources may be used to defeat the enemy. The central command then draws up a campaign plan that specifies which military units are to carry out which actions with which weaponry and stocks of ammunition (and clothing and supplies of food) and with which logistical support (which itself will be supplied in specified ways). The central command will then issue orders to its military personnel, full obedience to which will add up to carrying out the campaign plan. The officers in command of particular units may well not understand why they have been ordered to capture and hold the bridge at Arnhem – because they will not have the central command's Big Picture. Hence, the actions of particular military units can be successfully coordinated only if their officers get those units to perform their centrally assigned tasks.[17] Within designed social orders, the *law* that makes that order possible is a body of more or less specific commands to individuals that direct them in their assigned tasks within the designed order (1973: 49).

As an example of spontaneous *natural* order, consider an ecological order. At one time, it was thought that the extreme, intricate, and subtle connections between the elements of an ecological order must be evidence for its intelligent design and construction. It was thought that ecological order must be designed order. However, most people now understand ecological orders to be the continually evolving products of the interactions between and the mutual adaptions of their (surviving) component elements. The *laws* that make such a *natural* spontaneous order possible are not the commands of any ecological magistrate but, rather, the empirical biological and chemical laws that determine the consequences of particular factual situations within that order (as it evolves).

As one would expect, for Hayek, the most salient example of a spontaneous *social* order is the order of a private property/free market economy.[18] Crucially, such an economy functions only to the degree that widespread compliance with certain norms of conduct is expected. Whereas a planned economy is supposed to work through people's compliance with the particular and distinct instructions issued to them by the central planner, private property/free market economies work through people's compliance with general constraining norms of the sort articulated by Hume. Don't dispossess first possessors. Don't dispossess people of holdings acquired through freely contracted trade (or donation). Don't welch on contractual agreements. The expectation of general compliance with these norms provides people with incentives to identify resources worth possessing, to take possession of them, to invest in possessions, and to produce for and engage in trade and for increasingly elaborate contractual transactions. And those very economic activities generate the market prices that better inform those activities. The *law* that makes this economic order possible is the body of enforceable rules that codifies in more detail the basic Humean constraints on how individuals may pursue their own discrete ends when others may be affected. In *LLL*, Hayek calls this body of norms the "rules of just conduct." For Hayek, each individual's freedom is a matter of others' compliance with these rules of just conduct.[19] So, a "free society" is a society with a high degree of compliance with these principles of justice.

Hayek's complaint is against the "constructive rationalist" belief that "human institutions will serve human purposes only if they have been deliberately designed for these purposes ... [and] that we owe all beneficial institutions to design, and that only such design has made or can make them useful for our purposes" (1973: 8–9). He does not claim that all social orders – or even all desirable social orders – are spontaneous orders. Armies and planned military campaigns exist. The Salvation Army exists. Firms, orchestras, prisons, and monasteries exist. Top-down organization makes sense and is desirable when a significant number of people share a single end or hierarchy of ends and when there is a leader who is well-informed about how to marshal the energy and talents of these people toward the achievement of their common goal. "[T]he two kinds of order will regularly co-exist in every society of any degree of complexity." However,

> What ... we find in all free societies is that, although groups will join in organizations for the achievement of some particular ends, the co-ordination of the activities of all these separate organizations, as well as of the separate individuals, is brought about by the forces making for a spontaneous order. (1973: 46)

All sorts of organizations composed of people who share or who have committed themselves to a common purpose will exist within a society that is structured by general compliance with the rules of just conduct rather than organizational commands. It is precisely the freedom associated with general respect for these structuring norms that enables individuals to seek, create, and selectively subscribe to the diverse social and economic organizations that arise in such a spontaneous society. (Essentially the same claim is developed in Nozick's discussion of the framework for utopia in the last chapter of *ASU*.)

For Hayek the core social scientific error that has undermined the cause of liberty is the belief that desirable social and economic order must ultimately be designed and imposed by legal commands.

> The enemies of liberty have always based their argument on the contention that order in human affairs requires that some should give orders and others obey. Much of the opposition to a system of freedom under general laws arises from the inability to conceive of an effective co-ordination of human activities without deliberate organization by a commanding intelligence. (1960: 159)

Still, according to Hayek, one of the organizations that is likely to exist *within* any large-scale spontaneous society is government, the proper primary purpose of which is the refinement and enforcement of the rules of conduct that provide the framework for bottom-up social and economic coordination. "In a free society the state does not administer the affairs of men. It administers justice among men who conduct their own affairs."[20]

It is important to distinguish here between spontaneous orders that are composed of particular *concrete* facts and spontaneous orders that are composed of *abstract* rules. The vast array of particular economic states of affairs that would show up on a wide-angle snapshot of a free market economy, for example Jones' possession of this shovel and Smith having a particular contractual relationship with Brown, constitute a *concrete* spontaneous order. In contrast, the set of rules, general compliance with which makes this sort of concrete spontaneous order possible, is itself an *abstract* order. As another example, the set of abstract rules of a given language that makes possible the concrete *spontaneous* order that consists of all the linguistic interchanges among those employing that language, is itself an unplanned, evolved order. While Hayek notes that it is *possible* that such an abstract order of rules be the product of human design (1973: 46), it is highly unlikely that any genius (or committee of geniuses) sat around and thought up the rules, general compliance with which would facilitate the unintended production of the incredibly intricate and extensive concrete spontaneous order that constitutes a large-scale free market economy. It is similarly unlikely that the rules of any genuinely useful language were thought up by some brilliant linguistic engineer. Rather, the orders of rules through which concrete spontaneous orders emerge are themselves apt to be spontaneous orders, the unintended results of a process of cultural evolution.

> These rules of conduct have thus not developed as the recognized conditions for the achievement of a known purpose, but have evolved because the groups who practiced them were more successful and displaced others. (1973: 18)

> Although such rules come to be generally accepted because their observation produces certain consequences, they are not observed with the intention of producing those consequences – consequences which the acting person need not know. (1973: 19)

These evolved rules themselves embody information, not about current levels of scarcity and demand but rather about what patterns of interaction among human beings tend to lead to successful outcomes. According to Hayek, the evolution of individuals as agents disposed to abide by rules goes hand in hand with the evolution of social and economic orders that depend upon (and bestow the benefits of) rule compliance. For, a society's fitness for selection depends upon the degree to which its members are disposed to be rule compliant. This explains why "Man is as much a rule-following animal as a purpose-seeking one" (1973: 11).

Once we understand how such rules function to facilitate interaction among individuals to mutual social and economic advantage, we may investigate ways of deliberately improving these rules so that they become even more conducive to cooperation among individuals who "are allowed to use their knowledge for their purposes, restrained only by rules of just conduct of universal application" (1973: 55). However, we must always guard against the impulse to transgress such rules in particular cases for the sake of advancing some specific party's ends. We must always remind ourselves that we often are mistaken in our predictions of the consequences of particular interventions, that thwarting the utilization of local knowledge will on the whole be less beneficial than allowing such utilization (1960: 30–1), and that such transgressions undermine the systemic benefits that arise from the expectation of general compliance with the rules of just conduct.

In *LLL*, Hayek places special emphasis on the need not to undermine the general expectation that the rules of just conduct will be obeyed.

> [T]he rules which have been adopted because of their beneficial effects in the majority of cases will have these beneficial effects only if they are applied to all cases to which they refer, irrespective of whether it is known, or even true, that they will have a beneficial effect in the particular case. (1976: 16)

He then cites Hume's "classical exposition of the rationale for rules of justice."

> [H]owever single acts of justice may be contrary, either to public or private interest, it is certain that the whole plan or

scheme is highly conducive, or indeed, absolutely requisite, both to the support of society, and to the well-being of every individual. (1976: 155)

Any transgression of the norms that provide the framework for individual agents to utilize their particular knowledge to coordinate with one another to advance their respective purposes will undermine reliance upon that framework and, in diffuse ways that cannot be specifically predicted, will diminish the gains from such coordination. Moreover, even if there are particular cases in which transgressing the coordination-enhancing rules will be more beneficial than harmful, we do not have the factual information needed to identify those cases and limit our deviation from the generally beneficial rules to those cases. Worse yet,

> Any such restriction, any coercion other than the enforcement of general rules, will aim at the achievement of some foreseeable particular result, but what is prevented by it will usually not be known ... And so, when we decide each issue solely on what appear to be its individual merits, we always over-estimate the advantages of central direction ... If the choice between freedom and coercion is thus treated as a matter of expediency, freedom is bound to be sacrificed in almost every instance. ... freedom can be preserved only if it is treated as a supreme principle which must not be sacrificed for particular advantages. (1973: 57)

Individuals can treat freedom – the condition that obtains for all when there is general compliance with the rules of just conduct – as a supreme principle because we are as much rule-following animals as purpose-seeking ones. We must treat freedom as an ultimate value that need not be justified on a case-by-case basis if we are to reap the systematic benefits of assured reciprocal compliance with the rules of just conduct. The consequentialist argument on behalf of respect for freedom requires consequentialism's own transcendence.[21]

There is a further important element in Hayek's critique of central economic and societal planning. The standard conclusion of the Socialist Calculation argument is that, *even assuming that the central planners know what to plan for*, they will not be able to allocate resources rationally to achieve the plan's final goal. Hayek, however, also maintains that the central planners will not know what to plan for. For, they will not possess knowledge of the relative importance of all the different sorts of ends that they would have to weigh against one another to determine which overall social outcome should be promoted.

> Economic planning always involves the sacrifice of some ends in favour of others, a balancing of costs and results, a choice between alternative possibilities; and the decision always presupposes that all the different ends are ranged in a definite order according to their importance, an order which assigns to each objective a quantitative importance which tells us what sacrifices of other ends it is still worth pursuing and what price would be too high. (1997 [1939]: 210)

A planned or directed economic system,

> ... presupposes, in fact, the existence of something that does not exist and has never existed; a complete moral code in which the relative values of all human ends, the relative importance of all the needs of all the different people, are assigned a definite place and a definite quantitative significance. (1997 [1939]: 201–2)

The problem does not apply merely to economic planning. It applies to any justification for social policies – especially state-imposed social policies – on the grounds that the ends attained justify the sacrifice of the ends foregone. Constructivist rationalists are under the "illusion" that reason can "tell us what we ought to do" in the sense of revealing "common ends" that "all reasonable men ought to be able to join in the endeavor to pursue" (1973: 32). However, phrases like "social welfare," the "general interest," and "the common good" are empty formulas that provide no real guidance for any social choice of one concatenation of human ends over some other concatenation.

The plurality of ultimate ends to which distinct individuals are devoted cannot be transcended by attributing to these ends "a measureable common attribute for which either the term pleasure or the term utility was employed" (1976: 18).

For, according to Hayek, we lack knowledge of any such measurable common attribute.

> It is as much because we lack the knowledge of a common hierarchy of the importance of the particular ends of different individuals as because we lack the knowledge of particular facts, that the order of the Great Society must be brought about by the observance of abstract and end-independent rules. (1976: 39)

Thus, there is a further reason why a society composed (to revert to Rawls' language) of a "plurality of distinct persons with separate systems of ends" cannot be a centrally planned society. A rationally planned society needs to have a rationally identifiable shared substantive end or hierarchy of ends that is to be advanced by its plan. However, there is no such rationally detectible common end or weighted set of ends.

In fact, it is a great, albeit surprising, virtue of a free society that it has no unifying purpose toward the promotion of which its members are to march in step.

> [T]he cosmos of the market neither is nor could be governed by such a single scale of ends; it serves the multiplicity of separate and incommensurable ends of all its separate members. (1976: 108)

> A Great Society has nothing to do with, and is in fact irreconcilable with "solidarity" in the true sense of unitedness in the pursuit of known common ends. (1976: 111)

In *LLL*, Hayek is quite clear that the incommensurability of the value of people's individual ends rules out both act and rule versions of utilitarianism. For even the latter is committed to justifying the rules that it endorses on the basis of the particular outcomes that are expected to arise from compliance with those rules having a higher net score along some scale of ends than the particular outcomes of compliance with any other set of rules (1976: 3).

The rejection of a common societal purpose does not, of course, mean that the members of that society lack rational ends of their own. And it does not mean that the structure of a free society will not serve the purposes of its members. Rather, in a society structured by general compliance with the rules of just conduct (and other evolved and refined orders of rules), this abstract framework will be an instrument for each individual advancing her own purposes – often through freely chosen association with like-minded others. Nevertheless,

> Among the members of a Great Society, who mostly do not know each other, there will exist no agreement on the relative importance of their respective ends. There would exist not harmony but open conflict of interests if agreement were necessary as to which particular interests should be given preference over others. What makes agreement and peace in such a society possible is that the individuals are not required to agree on ends but only on means which are capable of serving a great variety of purposes and which each hopes will assist him in the pursuit of his own purposes. (1976: 3)

> The Great Society arose through the discovery that men can live together in peace and mutually benefiting each other without agreeing on the particular aims which they severally pursue. (1976: 109)

Given the plurality of distinct persons with their own systems of ends and our lack of knowledge about how to weigh people's diverse ultimate ends against one another, fundamental societal principles must take the form of distinguishing between the ways of advancing one's ends that are acceptable and the ways that are unacceptable. More specifically, conduct in accordance with norms that are conducive to peace and cooperation to mutual advantage – such as the rules of just conduct – are acceptable, while violations of those norms are unacceptable. Reciprocal compliance with such norms is each person's all-purpose means of advancing her own ends. This means will be available to each agent only if all are steadfast in their compliance (or are steadfastly punished for non-compliance). And all will be steadfast in their compliance (or steadfastly punished for non-compliance) only if these norms are treated as ultimate values. Respect for those values will be the "true common interest of the members of a Great Society, who do not pursue any particular common purpose" (1973: 121).

Still, why should one endorse reciprocal compliance with norms like the rules of just conduct even if it is granted that such an endorsement is "the indispensable foundation of all our civilization?" Why is it a "great tragedy" (1973: 7) when social scientific error undermines belief in strict compliance with such norms? The answer that is strongly suggested by Hayek's whole account of the function of such norms is that reciprocal compliance with such norms is apt to enhance the value of each participant's life from the perspective of her own distinct system of ends. The great virtue of the market order – indeed, the whole social order that arises from individual choices made within a framework of rules of just conduct – is that it "serves the multiplicity of separate and incommensurable ends of all its separate members" (1976: 108).

Three qualifications should be mentioned in connection with my conclusion that ultimately Hayek endorses a *mutual advantage* justification for compliance with the rules of just conduct. The first is that, while he does offer this justification, he also continues to be reluctant to acknowledge that he is doing so. This reluctance stems from his ongoing belief that to offer such a justification is to be guilty of overrating the power of human reason. The second qualification is that in *LLL*, Hayek construes the ultimate end that is served by compliance with the rules of just conduct in a slightly different way. In *LLL*, Hayek seems to think that, *if* he is to offer any sort of consequentialist justification for principles of action, he needs to point to some sort of outcome that is more *societal* than mutual benefit for each member of society. However, for reasons that we have discussed, that societal outcome cannot be the totality of particular concrete consequences of compliance with those principles. What Hayek comes up with is the idea that compliance with the rules of just conduct (and other coordinating norms) will always yield some particular instantiation of an "order of actions" in which individuals will live together in peace and mutually supportive interaction. While we cannot predict which particular instantiation of such an order will result from our compliance with the rules of just conduct, we can predict that *some* instantiation of a peaceful and mutually advantageous kind will emerge. So, if one needs to point to some sort of a societal end as the touchstone for rational policy, one should adopt this abstract end. "[R]ational policy" does not have access to and does not require "a common scale of concrete ends;" rather "policy ... may be directed toward the securing of an abstract overall order." Indeed, this abstract order is "a timeless purpose which will continue to assist ... individuals in the pursuit of their temporary and still unknown aims" (1976: 117, 14).[22]

The third qualification of my claim that Hayek ultimately appeals to mutual advantage is that Hayek will occasionally slip into more Kantian (and, hence, Nozickian) language. For instance, within *CL*, in which Hayek advances the consequentialist argument that we make the best use of one another by not coercing one another, he also declares that, "Coercion is evil [a term he *rarely* uses] precisely because it thus eliminates an individual as a thinking and valuing person and makes him a bare tool in the achievements of the ends of another." Hayek adds that justifiable coercion is coercion that suppresses initiated coercion and, hence, "becomes an instrument assisting individuals [who do not initiate coercion] in the pursuit of their own ends and not a means to be used [against individuals] for the ends of others" (1960: 21). This non-consequentialist rejection of coercion is, of course, a prelude to Hayek's insistence in *LLL* that freedom must be respected for its own sake if we are to reap the mutual gains that freedom promises.

4
Economic Justice and Property Rights

Introduction

This chapter focuses on libertarian stances on economic justice and property rights as these stances are articulated by Nozick and Hayek. Since most of the highbrow advocacy for extensive State power is for power that is to be directed toward the achievement of some vision of distributive justice, an important part of Nozick's and Hayek's defense of a minimal, or at least semi-minimal, State is their critiques of such visions of distributive justice and their contrasting arguments on behalf of robust private property rights. This focus on the rejection of coercive implementation of doctrines of distributive justice and on advocacy of private property and free market economic regime should not, of course, obscure libertarianism's comparable opposition to the extension of state action to the coercive suppression of displeasing, sinful, or self-harming conduct. Hayek well expresses the libertarian stance on these matters when he says,

> [T]he pleasure or pain that may be caused by the knowledge of other people's actions should never be regarded as a legitimate cause for coercion. ... [T]he mere dislike of what is being done by others, or even the knowledge that others harm themselves by what they do, provides no legitimate ground for coercion. (1960: 145)

Libertarian opposition to coercive measures on behalf of distributive justice may be based on the empirical contention that such measures are not necessary for the emergence of the desired distribution of income or even that such measures are likely to have undesired distributional results. It is often contended that the long-run operation of free market economics raises the income of the lower income members of society at least as much as the actual coercive measures that states pursue in the name of assisting the lower income members of society. Similarly, it is maintained that free market economies offer people more upward mobility and incentives to realize that mobility than highly regulated economies. I believe that these empirical claims are largely correct. However, substantiating these contentious factual claims goes beyond the philosophical scope of this book.

A more purely philosophical opposition to state coercive action aimed at promoting some favored distribution of income challenges the *conceptual* core of the case for such action, viz., that economic justice consists in the realization of some formulaic distribution of income among the members of society. Different advocates of this core claim have their own more specific views about what the correct distributive principle is, for example, the equality of income or the highest level of income for the lowest income group or the greatest correlation of individual income to personal desert. Particular opponents of distributional justice will often be especially interested in criticizing what they take to be the most seductive distributive principle. Nozick selects for special attention the Rawlsian view that economic justice consists in the promotion of the highest level of income for the lowest income individuals, while Hayek pays special attention to the view that individual income should correspond to personal moral desert. Nevertheless, the central philosophical objection offered by political libertarianism to the idea that economic justice demands coercive state intervention is that economic justice does not consist in the realization of *any* purported best division of income.

Nozick on Historical Entitlement, Property Rights, and the Lockean Proviso

Although Nozick labels his chapter on justice in holdings, "Distributive Justice," he notes that this phrase is not neutral among competing theories of economic justice (1974: 149). The phrase suggests that, *however an existing set of holdings has come about* within a given population, it is necessary to inquire whether there is some better or more just way for those holdings to be divided within (*or beyond*) that population. "Distributive justice" suggests that justice is a matter of identifying and applying some formula for measuring any existing set of holdings against other available divisions and determining whether the existing holdings should be allowed to stand or should be transformed into one of those alternative divisions *independent of how the existing holdings have come about*. Perhaps there is such a formula, and justice requires that we abide by its determinations. Nevertheless, it is illicit to build into one's terminology the assumption that the justice (or injustice) of holdings cannot derive from the way in which they have arisen. When Tom Brady, the New England Patriots quarterback, ends up with a much higher income from throwing footballs than I do, the justice of our very different holdings may have nothing to do with their distribution satisfying some formula for a just division of income and everything to do with people willingly paying more of their money to see Tom throw than to see me throw.

> In a free society, diverse persons control different resources, and new holdings arise out of the voluntary exchanges and actions of persons. There is no more distributing or distribution of shares than there is a distributing of mates in a society in which persons choose whom they shall marry. The total result is the product of many individual decisions which the different individuals involved are entitled to make. (1974: 149–50)

In addition to presupposing that the justice of a set of holdings depends on that set according with the demands of some distributionist formula, the demand for "distributive justice" presumes that there is some "person or group entitled to control all the resources, jointly deciding how they are to be doled out" (1974: 149). "Distributive justice" suggests that the total income within a society is a fortuitous social pie – a bundle of manna from heaven – that some authority has a right and a duty to divide (or re-divide) according to some favored distributional norm.

In contrast to these presumptions, Nozick outlines a "historical entitlement" theory of justice in holdings that makes the manner in which persons have come to possess their particular holdings determinative of the justice or injustice of those particular possessions. On Nozick's theory, individuals acquire rights to particular items (whatever their economic value may be) by obtaining them in entitlement generating ways and *ipso facto* acquire rights to the totality of the items acquired in these ways. The just claims of individuals to particular items do not consist in claims to certain "fair shares" of society's holdings. Rather, just acquisition is a type of game governed by rules about what one must do to acquire entitlements. If and only if one's acquisition arises through the performances that the rules deem to generate titles, does one gain an entitlement to the acquired object.

According to the rules of (American) football, there are various ways of scoring certain numbers of points – e.g., touchdowns, extra points, and field goals. By the end of the game, each team will be entitled to a certain total of points depending on how many times each performed diverse scoring plays. Suppose that one team ends up with 45 points and the other with 3 and someone raises the question of whether this was a just or fair distribution of points. Wouldn't it have been more just or fair if the scores had been more equal or if the scores were reversed because, after all, the team initially awarded 3 points did try awfully hard? According to Nozick's historical entitlement view, the appropriate response to such questions is that the only way to determine which team is entitled to how many points is for the game actually to be played; it is only through the actual playing of the game that entitlements to points accrue to the teams. The role of the referees is to enforce the general rules that constitute the game of football and, thereby, facilitate a good play of the game. The justice of the final holdings of points *emerges* from the rule-governed play of the game.[1]

Note how this approach accords with our day-to-day perspective about whether a given individual is (or is not) entitled to some particular holding, for example the earrings that she has been wearing. We ask questions about the *processes* through which this individual has come into possession of those earrings. Did she produce the earrings herself out of materials to which she was entitled? Did she purchase the earrings (or those materials) through a voluntary and honest transaction with their former possessor? If so, did the former possessor himself acquire these earrings (or those materials) through procedures that generated for him a right to them? Did the current purchaser acquire the funds for her purchase in a just fashion? We affirm the current possessor's right when we have satisfied ourselves about the provenance of that object. The current possessor's right to the earrings depends on her possession of the earrings having the proper sort of history – just as an individual's currently having a contractual right to another's performance depends upon the relevant contract having been actually and properly engaged.

There are three general ways in which an acquisition of some extra-personal object, for example, an acorn, a bit of arable land, a shovel, or a smartphone, can take place. First, one may acquire an unowned object, that is, a bit of raw material that has never been owned or an object that has been owned but is now abandoned. Second, one may acquire an object by transfer from its current possessor. Third, one may re-acquire an object that one has retained a right to, but which has come into the possession of another. (If one has retained the right to some object and it has been damaged or destroyed by another, one may "re-acquire" that object by extracting rectification payments from the party who damaged or destroyed it.) According to Nozick, a historical entitlement theory needs to specify what qualities acts of initial acquisition, acts of transfer, and acts of re-acquisition must have in order to engender (or preserve) entitlements in the resulting possessors to the items they have acquired.

The principle of justice in initial acquisition will articulate "the complicated truth" concerning the issues of how unheld things may come to be held, the process, or processes, by which unheld things may come to be held, the things that may come to be held by these processes, the extent of what comes to be held by a particular process, and so on. (1974: 150)

The principle of justice in transfer will articulate "the complicated truth" that answers the questions

> By what processes may a person transfer holdings to another? How may a person acquire a holding from another who holds it? Under this topic comes general descriptions of voluntary exchange, and gift and (on the other hand) fraud, as well as reference to particular conventional details fixed upon in a given society. (1974: 150)

A full statement of Nozick's procedural theory of justice in holdings would also articulate the complicated truth about the rectification of injustice in holdings.

> The general outlines of the theory of justice in holdings are that the holdings of a person are just if he is entitled to them by the principles of justice in acquisition and transfer, or by the principle of rectification of injustice (as specified by the first two principles). If each person's holdings are just, then the total set (distribution) of holdings is just. (1974: 153)

Nozick does not attempt to formulate these complicated truths. He does not offer "... a precise statement of the principles of the tripartite theory of distributive justice" (1974: xiv). I think that there are two reasons that Nozick does not worry about the details of his principles of just initial acquisition, just transfer, and just rectification. The first is that he sees his main task to be to establish that the overall historical entitlement approach is more plausible than the overall distributionist approach. The second is that he expects his readers to share with him an inventory of commonsense views about what procedures engender entitlements and what procedures do not. So, for instance, fashioning a tool of a new sort through difficult and sustained labor upon some widely available and unowned material gives rise to an entitlement to that tool, whereas naming a continent that has not previously been named (in a European language) does not engender an entitlement to that continent.

Nevertheless, there are issues here about the capacity of philosophical reasoning to identify one specific set of rules about just initial acquisition, transfer, and rectification[2] that constitute *the* complicated truths about just acquisition. Nozick himself expresses doubt about there being, "some set of principles obvious enough to be accepted by all men of good will, precise enough to give unambiguous guidance in particular situations, clear enough so that all will realize its dictates, and complete enough to cover all problems that actually arise" (1974: 141). Also, if in addition to philosophical reasoning, "conventional details" (1974: 150) are needed in the specification of any given society's rules for just acquisition, there are questions about how the specified rules possess the natural moral force that Nozick takes them to have. I will return to these issues in Chapter 5 when I consider Murphy and Nagel's critique of natural rights libertarianism.

The entitlement view is a bottom-up view of justice in holdings. The basic instances of just holdings are the particular just holdings of particular individuals (or associations of individuals) – Ben's possession of this acorn, Jen's possession of that bit of arable land. The totality of the holdings among the members of a given society will be just insofar as the particular holdings of those members are just. To determine whether and to what degree the totality of the holdings within a society is just or unjust, one has to start at the level of particular holdings of particular agents and examine the pedigree of those holdings. If all the particular holdings of all particular agents are just on the basis of their respective just pedigrees, the totality of holdings in that society is just – *whatever overall profile or pattern of holdings among those agents obtains or fails to obtain*.

In contrast, on all distributionist doctrines, the justice of the extent of the holdings of a particular individual (or association) is dependent upon the justice of the societal distribution of which it is a component. The justice of any given agent's holding flows downward to that holding from the justice of the total allocation of holdings in that society. On any distributionist view, the justice of the overall array of holdings in society and, thereby, the justice of each component of that array will be the intended consequence of institutions and policies that are designed to bring about the favored overall distribution. In contrast, on the historical entitlement view, the overall array of holdings *and its justice* will be unintended consequences of individuals (and associations) being free to procure and retain holdings in accordance with just procedures of acquisition.

Nozick distinguishes between two types of distributionist doctrines. There are "end-state" doctrines and there are "pattern" doctrines. Each end-state doctrine offers a formula for ranking alternative available distributions of income among individuals (or households). Consider the following available distributions:

	A	B	C
Distribution D$_1$	12	10	9
Distribution D$_2$	4	22	13
Distribution D$_3$	20	8	8

A utilitarian distributionist (focusing on income rather than utility) will rank D$_2$ highest on the ground that it has the greatest total income. An egalitarian distributionist will rank D$_1$ highest on the ground that it is the most equal distribution. A fan of Rawls' difference principle will rank D$_1$ highest on the distinct ground that its lowest payoff is greater than the lowest payoff within any other available distribution. What makes each of these doctrines an end-state view is their shared conviction that the information provided by this sort of matrix is sufficient for determining which of the available distributions is the best (and, hence, the just) one.

According to Nozick, a deep problem for all end-state doctrines is the falsity of this shared conviction. For, surely information that *cannot* appear within such a matrix is essential to any sensible judgment about which of these distributions merits endorsement. Among the information that cannot appear within such a matrix is information about what means will have to be employed or what basic structures will have to be maintained in order to realize these alternative outcomes. Consider the following information. D$_2$ is the distribution of income that arises when A is enslaved to B who employs C as his effective overseer. D_1 is the distribution that arises when A is partially emancipated and is only subject to slavery-like exploitation by B and C one week per month. And D_3 is the distribution that arises when A is entirely emancipated. Thus, to opt for D_2 is to opt for the means-structure of full-fledged slavery. To opt for D_1 is to opt for the means-structure of partial slavery. Only by opting for D_3 does one avoid opting for some degree of slavery. Given the obvious relevance of this sort of information for any responsible selection of one of these distributions as the just one, any doctrine that asserts or presumes that the information available in such a matrix suffices for a responsible selection has to be deeply flawed. Note that this is not a *distributionist* argument for D_3 being the best of the three allocations. It is an argument for attending to means – to procedures – rather than outcomes (which are all that can be reported in the matrices of the end-stater). D_3 will be the just outcome if and only if, under the non-slavery structure, D_3 actually emerges from the free choices of just interactions made by A, B, and C.

The second sort of distributionist approach identified by Nozick is the pattern approach. According to this approach, distributions of income among agents ought to map on to the distribution of some normatively significant trait of those agents. Each specific pattern theory selects some specific trait as the trait that income should track. The available distribution that best tracks the selected trait is the just distribution. A pattern theorist might select depth of religious conviction, steadfastness of political loyalty, or degree of moral virtue as the basis for receipt of income. Since information about the distribution of any of these traits cannot be found within the end-stater's matrices, the pattern theorist cannot be charged with thinking that the sensible ranking of available distributions of income can proceed entirely on the basis of the information found within such matrices.

Pattern doctrines can be either non-historical or historical. A *non-historical* pattern doctrine will track a trait that exists in varying degrees in individuals at the time that shares of income are being assigned. For instance, the view that the just distribution is the available distribution that most allots income to individuals in proportion to their IQs is a non-historical pattern doctrine. No non-historical pattern seems even minimally plausible. A *historical* pattern doctrine will track a trait that has been manifested in varying degrees by individuals for some period preceding the allocation of income shares. For instance, the view that the just distribution is the distribution that most allots income to individuals in proportion to their moral desert is a historical pattern doctrine. Any advocate of a historical pattern view will agree with Nozick that all end-state views are defective because they fail to attend to *historical* information that is not revealed in the end-stater's matrices. However, there remains a crucial difference between any historical *pattern* view and the historical entitlement approach. The historical information that the latter takes to be determinative of the justice or injustice of particular holdings (and, hence, of arrays of such holdings) is information about the *processes by which that set of holdings has arisen*, not information about what pattern of the selected *trait* has obtained among the individuals to whom income is to be proportionately distributed.

Due to this difference, Nozick's manna from heaven complaint still applies to historical pattern theories. For, according to any such theory, the justice or injustice of particular holdings will not be determined by the actual historical processes that have produced those particular holdings. Rather, the totality of existing holdings are, for the purposes of justice in holdings, treated as simply available – again, like manna from heaven – to be sliced up or re-sliced according to some favored formula.

> To think that the task of a theory of distributive justice is to fill in the blank in "to each according to his _____" is to be predisposed to search for a pattern, and the separate treatment of "from each according to his _____" treats production and distribution as two separate and independent issues. On an entitlement view these are *not* two separate questions. (1974: 159–60)

Of course, the sensible application of any such distributionist formula will take account of the effect of that application on future production and, hence, on what distributions will be available in the future – as does Rawls' application of the difference principle. However, this attention to the factual consequences of the application of a distributionist principle is fundamentally different from taking productive (or destructive) processes as themselves morally significant in determining the justice or injustice of the results of those processes.

Two of the most important sections of Nozick's chapter on "Distributive Justice" offer further criticisms that apply to both end-state and to pattern doctrines. (In these sections Nozick uses the term "pattern" to refer to both main types of distributionist approach.) The first of these is "How Liberty Upsets Patterns" (1974: 160–4). The title of this section may have contributed to the false impression that Nozick's argument against pattern views is simply that liberty is in conflict with the maintenance of patterns and, since liberty should be favored, patterns should be disfavored. This impression is reinforced when Nozick says that his basic contention "is that no end-state principle or distributional patterned principle of justice can be continuously realized without continuous interference with people's lives" (1974: 163). However, were this Nozick's argument, any distributionist could equally well say that, once one realizes that liberty upsets patterns, one sees how readily one should be prepared to upset liberty. For Nozick's argument against patterns not to be question begging on behalf of liberty, he needs to reveal important difficulties *within* the advocacy of patterns. I shall explain how Nozick accomplishes this.

In "How Liberty Upsets Patterns," Nozick deploys two nice examples. The first example involves a million fans of basketball player Wilt Chamberlain each paying Wilt an extra 25 cents out of their just distributional share of income for the pleasure of watching him play. The second involves an individual living within a socialist society who utilizes portions of (what the advocate of this society deems to be) his just distributional share and his leisure time to enhance his income through capitalist acts with consenting adults. In both cases, individuals freely deploying resources to which they are said to have just distributive claims upset what is said to be the just distribution of resources. I will employ a different, more complex, and less entertaining example that,

I believe, serves a more precise statement of the internal difficulties that Nozick ascribes to all distributionist doctrines.

Nozick invites each of his distributionist interlocutors to imagine that the available distribution of income (in the form of currency or other economically valuable holdings) that she herself takes to be just has been brought into existence. For the sake of working through Nozick's critique, let us assume that this favored formula is the ever-popular difference principle. And let us assume that the three distributions that are depicted in the next matrix are available for a society composed of four individuals[3] A, B, C, and D.

	A	B	C	D
Distribution D_4	24	25	26	27
Distribution D_5	27	27	30	37
Distribution D_6	26	32	34	42

On the basis of the difference principle, our distributionist will rank D_5 highest and deem it to be the just distribution. Let us suppose, then, that D_5 is instituted. Nozick's question is: what then?

His answer is that almost certainly some of these individuals will deploy resources that have been assigned to them in the name of justice in highly innocuous ways that will create new distributions that will have to be declared to be unjust by the very formula for distributive justice that assigned those resources to them in the name of justice. Here is a simple illustration of such an individual's innocuous deployment of justly assigned resources creating a new distribution that will have to be declared to be unjust. C, working on his own, transforms some raw timber that makes up three units of his just holdings within D_5 into a quaint tiny house that has a value of 18 units. Taking account of his loss of the raw timber and the three-unit cost to him involved in his labor, C's net income rises to 42. Through this productive activity C brings a new distribution into existence, $D_5{}^*$ – one that does not at all affect anyone else's "legitimate share" (1974: 161) under D_5. However, once $D_5{}^*$ comes into existence, yet another distribution is almost certain to become available, for example, D_7 (as specified below), which the difference principle ranks higher than D_5^*. For, almost certainly, it will be possible to convert D_5^* into D_7 by imposing a new ("windfall") tax on C that will redistribute some of his enhanced income to A and to B (and cover the administrative costs of doing so). Hence, the available distributions become:

	A	B	C	D
Distribution D_5^*	27	27	42	37
Distribution D_7	29	29	36	37

Given the availability of D_7, D_5^* *must be declared to be unjust by the very same distributive principle that, in the name of justice, required the selection of D_5 over D_4 and D_6.*

Yet, Nozick asks, how could the sort of innocuous activity engaged in by C introduce injustice into the society in question? How can the distributionist who insists on the justice of D_5 maintain that the introduction of C's *productive activity* transforms the economic order under examination from a just one into an unjust one? The holdings of A, B, and D are not affected by C's productive enhancement of his own income;[4] so, if those holdings were just before C's self-generated gain, how could that gain have rendered them unjust? Writing about the Wilt Chamberlain case, in which a departure from the established just distribution takes place through exchange, Nozick asks,

> By what process could such a transfer among two persons give rise to a legitimate claim of distributive justice on a portion of what was transferred [or on a portion of what was not transferred], by a third party who had no claim of justice on any holding of the others *before* the transfer. (1974: 161–2)

The distributionist may be tempted to say that the answer is obvious. Injustice is introduced because a departure from the pattern is introduced. However, this response is really a refusal to address Nozick's challenge; the response simply begs the question on behalf of the view that justice is always a matter of conformity to some favored distributionist formula.

The distributionist might offer a different answer to Nozick's challenge. She might say that C's activity is not innocuous or not just and, hence, D_5^* is not the upshot of a just starting-point combined with an innocuous or not unjust action; hence, it is no surprise that D_5^* is not just. But, on what ground can the distributionist say that C's activity is not innocuous or not just? It seems that the only ground the distributionist can give is that C's activity introduces a departure from D_5 which is, after all (by hypothesis), a just distribution. However, any appeal to this ground for judging C's activity to be non-innocuous or not just must radically restrict what C – and, indeed, all individuals – are entitled to do with resources that are said to be among their respective just holdings. No one will be entitled to deploy their justly held resources in a way that is disruptive of the distribution of resources within which their allotment of holdings counts as just.

However, Nozick contends, if what one may do with the objects that are said to be one's just holdings is restricted in this way, one is getting a lot less than it sounds like one is getting when one is allotted those holdings as one's just share. "[W]hat was [the distribution] for if not to do something with?" (1974: 161). It turns out that "Patterned distributional principles do not give people what entitlement principles do only better distributed. For they do not give the right to choose what to do with what one has" (1974: 167). It is not that our C will be *forbidden* to convert his raw timber into a much more valuable tiny house. It's that he may have to sell the tiny house to pay the tax bill he will receive for his injudicious use of what has been declared to be his just holding. Any distributionist stance will require continuous interference with *people peacefully doing as they choose with what has been declared to be their just holdings*. As Hillel Steiner puts it, ongoing applications of distributionist principles "create rights to interfere with the exercise of the rights they create" (1976: 43). This is a necessary consequence of *ongoing* adherence to any pattern. For, as Hayek would especially emphasize, the planners of the institutions and policies that are supposed to yield the fullest realization of some favored pattern will never be able to anticipate the ways in which individuals will discover and pursue opportunities for unilateral or cooperative improvement of their economic conditions within the regimes endorsed by those planners. (Also see "Rawls' Critique of Libertarianism" in Chapter 5.)

Let us return for a moment to our original set of alternative distributions in order to consider a possible objection to the libertarian (especially Nozickian) stance that has been expounded in this and the last chapter.

	A	B	C
Distribution D₁	12	10	9
Distribution D₂	4	22	13
Distribution D₃	20	8	8

Suppose that the actual distribution of holdings that has come into being (through A's enslavement to B) is D_2. The libertarian will declare this actual distribution to be unjust while also maintaining that, were D_3 to have arisen (through A's emancipation), it would be just. The objection will then be that the libertarian is engaged in precisely the sort of ranking of alternative social outcomes and trade-offs across persons that he prides himself in attacking. In the case at hand, the libertarian will be charged with saying that it is socially worthwhile for A to gain of 16 even at the cost of 14 for B and 5 for C. However, this objection is misplaced. The libertarian is *not* saying that D_3 is better than D_2. He is *not* engaged in ranking alternative social outcomes. Rather, he is saying that, when D_2 arises *through the unjust practice of slavery*, it is unjust in virtue of the injustice of its genesis whereas, were D_3 to arise *through interactions within a society of fully emancipated individuals*, D_3 would be just in virtue of its just genesis.

Nozick's section on "Redistribution and Property Rights" (1974: 167–74) also targets all versions of the distributionist approach. The key argument in this section turns on Nozick's implicit adherence to (something akin to) the self-ownership thesis according to which each individual has rights over her own mental and physical powers, talents, time, and efforts.

> When end-result principles of distributive justice are built into the legal structure of a society, they (as do most patterned principles) give each citizen an enforceable claim to some portion of the total social product; that is, to some portion of the sum total of the individually and jointly made products.

This total product is produced by individuals laboring, using means of production others have saved to bring into existence, by people organizing production or creating means to produce new things or things in a new way. It is on this batch of individual activities that patterned distributional principles give each individual an enforceable claim. (1974: 171–2)

Whether it is done through taxation on wages or on wages over a certain amount, or through seizures of profits, or through there being a big *social pot* so that it's not clear what's coming from where and what's going where, patterned principles of distributive justice involve appropriating the actions of other persons. ... This process ... makes them a *part-owner* of you; it gives them a property right in you. Just as having such partial control and power of decision, by right, over an animal or inanimate object would be to have a property right in it. ... These principles involve a shift from the classical liberal notion of self-ownership to a notion of (partial) property rights in *other* people. (1974: 172)

Only a historical entitlement system that recognizes the rights of individuals to the fruits of their faculties, talents, time, and energy – including whatever fruits of others' labor individuals acquire from others through voluntary exchange (or donation) – can avoid institutionalizing unconsented to infringements upon persons' self-ownership rights.

Here, too, Nozick does not specify the procedures through which particular individuals acquire property rights to specific items. He does not argue that the enforcement of any distributional pattern will violate at least some of those property rights that will have arisen through those specified, rights-generating procedures. Rather, he simply maintains that individuals who are subjected to schemes of taxation to which they do not as individuals consent are treated as though they are (in some respects) the property of those who impose or sponsor that taxation. Suppose the agents of individuals *E* and *F* follow around individuals *G* and *H* to keep track of the incomes that they generate by their peaceful unilateral and cooperative interactions, and demand that *G* and *H* each hand over a specified percentage of their income to those agents each April 15. If either fails to comply, the relevant percentage of her income or more will be seized and the miscreant may be whipped or imprisoned.

One way of criticizing this institution would be to explain precisely how G and H, through their various peaceful actions, have acquired property rights over the items those agents demand from them. Another way – which Nozick offers in "Redistribution and Property Rights" – is to observe that this taxation procedure makes G and H the *partial slaves* of those agents or their principals. Suppose that G and H in fact started out as full slaves of E and F. But these owners realized that they could increase their gains from their slaves by allowing them to fend for themselves (utilizing all of their local knowledge) and merely sending their tax-collecting agents to visit G and H on April 15. Isn't it clear that G and H would still be (at least) the partial slaves of E and F?[5] Can't one reach this conclusion without providing a specific account of how G and H acquired property rights to the possessions that the agents now seize?

Suppose, on the contrary, one holds that G and H are (without their actual consent) properly subject to a tax scheme that accords with one's favorite distributionist formula. Can one *still* hold that G and H have a right to emigrate into a lower tax or no tax territory? Members of the liberal intelligentsia typically affirm robust rights of emigration. Indeed, any denial by the distributionist of the rights of G and H to emigrate will bolster the contention that the tax scheme treats G and H as partial slaves. For, a denial of this right amounts to an endorsement of their *captivity*.[6] So, Nozick expects that the distributionist will want to affirm that individuals G and H have rights to emigrate even from a nation that has institutionalized that distributionist's favorite principle (1974: 173). Nozick then argues that, if one holds that G and H should be allowed to escape non-consensual taxation by migrating to other regions of the world, one must also hold that they should be allowed to engage in internal emigration. If people are to be permitted to leave their home territory in order to avoid such a tax scheme, then mustn't they be permitted to disengage from that tax scheme (and its putative benefits) without having to move to another region of the world?

What rationale yields the result that the person be permitted to emigrate, yet forbidden to stay and opt out of the compulsory scheme of social provision? If providing for the needy is of overriding importance, this does militate against allowing internal opting out; but it also speaks against allowing external emigration. (1974: 173)

An opponent of internal emigration may appeal to the slogan, "Love it or leave it." This, however, would put her in company that she would normally distain. More importantly, why must one leave it not to love it? Why must one leave in order to escape from what it would be permissible for one to escape by leaving? If individuals have a right to ignore the state that currently imposes a distributionist tax scheme on them by moving to a different territory, don't they also have a right to ignore the state's demand that they move in order to be ignored?[7] I can report that the force of this rhetorical question does drive friends of the difference principle to *deny* the right of productive individuals to emigrate. The argument then offered is the same as that offered by the Soviet Union on behalf of its holding its talented people in captivity, viz., the *state*'s investment in the raw human material under its control gives the *state* a right to the talents and skills it creates through that investment. Is this argument not equally available to the slave owner who has fed, lodged, and trained up from childhood his now highly skilled slave and now claims a right against the slave's escape?

Finally, Nozick introduces "an additional bit of complexity into the structure of the entitlement theory" (1974: 174). This is a proviso that is akin to Locke's "enough, and as good" proviso. Or at least it "satisfies the intent behind" (1974: 177) that proviso. As we have seen in chapter 2, Locke was concerned about whether the increased incentive for appropriating raw natural material that will be present in an advanced market society will lead to so much initial acquisition of raw material that "enough, and as good" will not be left for others. I suggested in Chapter 2 that the real issue for Locke is whether the increased and intensified privatization that is present in market societies will "straiten" anyone, that is, leave that person with less opportunity to bring her self-owned powers to bear in the pursuit of her ends than she would have were private property not to have developed (or had been coercively limited in its development). Since losing particular opportunities to be the initial acquirer of some raw material or even losing *all* opportunity to be the *initial* acquirer of any raw material need not leave one with less overall opportunity to bring one's powers to bear in the pursuit of one's ends, even the privatization of all raw material need not straiten one.

Nozick maintains that the vast increase in types of skills that become valuable within an elaborate market economy, and in the ways that one can acquire or use improved material resources through purchase, lease or employment, and the ways in which a highly decentralized economic order make it possible for individuals to find – or create – niches that mine their own special knowledge and talents, make it likely that everyone's opportunities will be greater than they would have been had private property not developed (or had been coercively limited). Such considerations are not intended "as a utilitarian justification of property" (1974: 177). Rather, they function to show why "the free operation of a market system will not actually run afoul of the Lockean proviso" (1974: 182).[8]

In characterizing the Lockean proviso proposed by Nozick, I have drawn upon Locke's idea that an individual will have a complaint in justice if the acquisitions of others (along with their decisions about how to utilize their legitimately acquired holdings) will "straiten" that individual, and the idea that a person is straitened when she is so hedged in by others' holdings (and their decisions about how to utilize those holdings) that her opportunities fall below the baseline of opportunities she would have were private property not to develop (or to be restricted in its development). I have expressed the Lockean proviso in terms of individuals not being made worse off in terms of opportunity.[9] In contrast, Nozick himself seems to have thought of his proviso more as a requirement that individuals not be made worse of in terms of their utility or welfare; the proviso is violated if and only if "the benefits of civilization [do] not counterbalance being deprived of ... particular liberties."[10]

Hayek on Social Justice versus the True Function of Market Remuneration

Like Nozick, Hayek sets to reject all distributionist doctrines. "Our objection is against all attempts to impress upon society a deliberately chosen pattern of distribution, whether it be an order of equality or of inequality" (1960: 87). Distributionist doctrines all presume that the experts in institutional and policy design can accurately inform us about what arrays of concrete results will be generated by alternative packages of institutions and policies. The experts are presumed to be able to predict that policy package P_1 will yield something pretty close to distribution D_1, package P_2 will yield something pretty close to D_2, and so on. This (presumed) knowledge enables those in authority to employ their favored distributional formula to identify which of the available distributions ranks highest and *ipso facto* which of the available policy packages ought to be selected.

As we have seen, however, Hayek holds that no social science expert will have sufficient factual information about individuals, their dispositions, skills, interests, preferences, or choices in order to predict what will be the arrays of particular results for those diverse individuals of instituting those various packages of institutions and policies.

> Nor can the choice of the appropriate set of rules be guided by balancing for each alternative set of rules considered the particular predictable favourable effects against the particular unfavourable effects, and then selecting the set of rules for which the positive net result is greatest [or most in accord with a favored distributionist formula]; for most of the effects on particular persons adopting one set of rules rather than another are not predictable. (1976: 3)

The relevant authorities will not know what distributions will result from which packages of institutions and policies and, therefore, they will not know what the available distributions are. In addition, Hayek maintains that, even if we knew what sets of concrete outcomes were available to us through the adoption of different bundles of institutions and policies, we would lack knowledge of a standard of value that would allow us to rank those sets of concrete outcomes against one another.

An appreciation of our factual ignorance about particular outcomes and our moral ignorance of a formula for ranking sets of particular outcomes combine with our understanding of how general compliance with the rules of just conduct is likely to serve all of our diverse interests – albeit, not in concretely predictable ways – to provide a strong rationale for compliance with and even enforcement[11] of those rules. They combine to yield an understanding of why it is vitally important to treat such rules as principles of justice "whose application *to particular instances* requires no justification" (1973: 61, emphasis added).[12] The key way in which general abidance with the rules of justice conduct assists individuals in their pursuit of their respective aims is that it enables each individual to make use of her own detailed local knowledge and the information available to her in the form of market prices *and* to benefit from others' use of their detailed local knowledge and the information that is available to them in the form of market prices.

These Humean–Hayekian rules are constraining norms. They require agents not to dispossess others of their legitimate initial acquisitions or their legitimate acquisitions through voluntary transfers and not to welch on validly formed contracts. Rules that are protective of property – indeed, property in the broad sense of life, liberty, and estate – are an essential means by which individuals can attain their respective ends because property is essential to individuals having incentives to develop, refine, and act upon their local knowledge about their own potentialities, the resources available to them, and their own and their prospective trading partners' desires.

> [M]en can use their own knowledge in the pursuit of their own ends without colliding with each other only if clear boundaries are drawn between their respective domains of free action. ... Property, in the wide sense in which it is used to include not only material things, but (as John Locke defined it) the "life, liberty and estates" of every individual, is the only solution men have yet discovered to the problem of reconciling individual freedom with the absence of conflict.[13] (1973: 107)

Hayek recognizes that, for property to arise, further rules are needed that specify the procedures through which things become owned by this or that agent. "[R]ules are required which make it possible at each moment to ascertain the boundary of the protected domain of each and thus to distinguish between the *meum* and the *tuum*" (1973: 107). These rules – like Nozick's complicated truths concerning just acquisition – specify "the manner in which such domains are acquired, transferred, lost, and delimited" (1976: 35). Nevertheless, Hayek shies away from labeling these modes of legitimate acquisition and transfer as rules of just conduct (1976: 35). According to Hayek, acquisition through the specified procedures establishes ownership; but ownership merits protection only because of the Humean rules of just conduct that bestow protection on people's established domains.

> Such states of 'ownership' [i.e., being acquired by legitimate, ownership-engendering procedures] have no significance *except through the rules of just conduct which refer to them*; leave out those rules of just conduct which refer to ownership, and nothing remains of it. (1976: 35, emphasis added)

Shortly we will see why Hayek declines to include the specification of the procedures through which individuals establish ownership among the principles of just conduct.[14]

In *MSJ*, Hayek offers a medley of arguments against distributive or social justice. I will survey five of these arguments: the Meaninglessness Argument, the Desert is Unknown Argument, the Signal Argument, the No Authority Argument, and the Political Dynamic Argument. I also consider a more positive proposal from *CL*, the Desert as Contribution Proposal.

The Meaninglessness Argument

This is Hayek's favorite argument against distributionism. According to this argument, it is *meaningless* to ascribe *injustice* to the distribution of income that arises within an economic order that is at least substantially based upon private property and free market interactions. "[I]n a society of free men (as distinct from any compulsory organization) the concept of social justice is strictly empty and meaningless" (1976: 68). Assertions of the injustice of the distribution of incomes *within such an economic order* do not even rise to the level of meaningful falsehoods. According to Hayek, there is a category mistake involved in saying that the distributional upshot of the operation of a (more or less) market order is unjust; for injustice is not a characteristic that is applicable to such an order. To ascribe injustice to the array of incomes that arise within a market order is like ascribing greenness to a quadratic equation. Hayek recognizes that there is a parallel argument for the conclusion that it is meaningless to assert the *justice* of any distribution of incomes that arises within a market order. He is willing to bear the intellectual cost of being excluded from meaningfully asserting the *justice* of market outcomes in order to gain the intellectual reward of excluding distributionists from meaningfully asserting the *injustice* of market outcomes.

Hayek expresses the crucial premise of the Meaninglessness Argument in two distinct ways. The first expression is that no outcome can be unjust unless some agent is blameworthy for that outcome.

> Strictly speaking, only human conduct [or, say, the conduct of God] can be called just or unjust. If we apply the terms to a state of affairs, they have meaning only in so far as we hold someone responsible for bringing it about or allowing it to come about. ... To apply the term 'just' [or 'unjust'] to circumstances other than human actions or the rules governing them is a category mistake. (1976: 31)

> Only if we mean to blame a personal creator does it make sense to describe it as unjust that somebody has been born with a physical defect, or has been stricken with a disease, or has suffered the loss of a loved one. Nature can be neither just nor unjust. (1976: 31–2)

When we see that there is no agent who is to blame for that defect or disease or loss, we withdraw our judgment that this defect or disease or loss is unjust. Similarly, when we overcome our habit of thinking "animistically or anthropomorphically" (1976: 32) about the array of incomes that arise within a market order, we withdraw any judgment that this array is unjust. We already see here the second premise of the Meaninglessness Argument, viz.,

> In a spontaneous order the position of each individual is the result of the actions of many other individuals, and nobody has the responsibility or the power to assure that these separate actions of many will produce a particular result for a certain person. (1976: 33)

The first expression of crucial premise combines with the second premise to yield the conclusion that the distribution of incomes that arises within a market economy can never intelligibly be described as unjust (or as just).

Why not, however, adopt the view we have seen in Nozick? According to that view, particular holdings that arise through legitimate means of acquisition are themselves just; and particular holdings that arise through other means are themselves not just; and a distribution of holdings is just insofar and only insofar as the particular holdings within it are just. Hayek takes this proposal to be "tempting." But he rejects it on the grounds that the overall array of holdings that arises within a spontaneous order will not be "the intended aim of the individual actions" (1976: 33). We saw above that Hayek declines to include the rules of legitimate acquisition among the rules of just conduct. I surmise that he does so because, had he classified these rules of acquisition as principles of justice, it would have been harder yet for him to resist the tempting conclusion that particular holdings that arise in accordance with those rules of acquisition are themselves just (and holdings that arise through other procedures are not just.)

The second expression of the key first premise of the Meaninglessness Argument is, "[I]f it is not the intended or foreseen result of somebody's action that A should have much and B little, this cannot be called just or unjust" (1976: 33). I take this to be a second expression of the *same* key premise because Hayek seems to hold that one is not responsible for an outcome of one's action if and only if that outcome is neither intended nor foreseen. We can also restate the second premise as the claim that no array of holdings that arises in a market economy is the intended or foreseen result of any agent's actions. And if we conjoin this expression of the key premise and this restatement of the second premise, we again arrive at the conclusion that the distribution of income that emerges within a market economy cannot be described as just or unjust.

Unfortunately for the Meaninglessness Argument, neither expression of the first key premise is correct. Consider the case of a rolling pin that has been legitimately acquired by Jerry but which quite accidentally gets dislodged from its place in Jerry's kitchen and rolls downhill into Bob's kitchen. It rolls right into the spot where Bob's identical rolling pin normally lies; so Bob takes it to be his own rolling pin. In this case, no one is to blame for Bob's possession of Jerry's rolling pin. Yet Bob's possession of it is unjust even though Bob does not realize this. When the facts of the matter become known, it is clear that justice requires that Bob return the pin to Jerry. Also, Bob's possession of the pin is not the intended or foreseen result of Bob leaving his kitchen door open; but it is nevertheless unjust. Consider now a slightly more complex example. Imagine a society of five individuals who, over the course of many years, acquire holdings of the extent indicated by D_8 in the matrix below and do so entirely on the basis of rules of acquisition that Hayek would deem to be legitimate (albeit, not just). But then individuals K and L retire from their honest economic endeavors and each, with no knowledge of the other, takes up his retirement plan of being a successful (undetected) pickpocket. Each proceeds in this vocation for a while and the upshot is D_9.

	H	I	J	K	L
Distribution D_8	18	27	13	16	14
Distribution D_9	15	19	11	22	19

No one agent or set of coordinated agents is blameworthy for D_9 (although K and L are blameworthy for certain of the losses suffered by H, I, and J). And no one agent or set of coordinated agents brings about D_9 intentionally or even with foresight. Yet it seems entirely reasonable to say that, compared to D_8, D_9 is a thoroughly, if not absolutely, unjust distribution. It seems entirely reasonable to say that through the actions of K and L considerable injustice has entered into this five-person society. When I, H, and J figure out what has been going on, they demand (at the very least) that K and L return the *unjust* components of their holdings. Thus, each of these examples shows that the key premise of the Meaninglessness Argument is mistaken.

If the Meaninglessness Argument has a saving grace, it is that it warns us about the tendency of doctrines of social justice to personify society as "a personal distributing agent whose will or choice determines the relative position of different persons or groups" (1976: 72) and whose will or choice will be just only if it is effectively directed toward the deliberate creation of some putatively best available distribution. Still, given its deep flaws, Hayek would lose little by jettisoning the Meaninglessness Argument. And he would gain a lot. For he could then embrace the historical entitlement view that *just* holdings can arise from individuals acquiring objects in accordance with just procedures even if the array or distribution of those holdings is not intended by anyone. He could hold, as Nozick does, that justice in holdings is among the welcome states of affairs that can arise without being intended.

The Desert is Unknown Argument

In *CL* Hayek takes *the* complaint of the supporter of social justice to be "that differences in reward do not correspond to any recognizable differences in the merits of those who receive them" (1960: 93). And this identification of "social justice" with the demand that income correspond with moral merit continues throughout *MSJ*. In this context, Hayek takes merit to be a matter of painful effort directed toward some beneficial result. However, Hayek's selection of distribution according to merit as the paradigm social justice view is odd. For, the demand that remuneration accord with individual merit is usually offered *in opposition to* social justice demands for the downward redistribution of income. At least by the time that *MSJ* was published, advocacy of downward redistribution was typically based on *end-state* principles such as Rawls' difference principle and not on *pattern* principles such as distribution according to merit.[15] So why does Hayek select distribution according to personal desert – and, more specifically, according to painful effort – as his primary target?

In *MSJ* Hayek maintains that old-fashioned socialists advocated central economic planning because they thought that this was the necessary route to their ultimate goal, viz., "a 'just' distribution of wealth." But new-fashioned socialists have "discovered that this redistribution could in great measure, and against less resistance [than central planning would face], be brought about by taxation"[16] (1976: 65). My suspicion is that Hayek assumes that the more direct attainment of distributive justice favored by the new-fashioned socialist must involve *a plan for the allocation of income* that requires the same degree of detailed information as *a plan for the productive allocation of economic resources* must involve. The distributionist view that fits Hayek's presumption that advocacy of distributive justice requires such a detailed, information-intensive plan is the view that just distribution is allocation in proportion to personal desert. Moreover, Hayek must have been heartened by the conclusion that the distributionist seeks allocation according to personal merit. For, this is the distributionist program that is most subject to Hayek's favorite general critique, viz., the program requires unattainable knowledge of particular matters of fact.

According to Hayek, the determination of any given individual's degree of merit – understood as the extent of painful effort directed toward beneficial results – is extraordinarily difficult. It is much more difficult than determining the degree of an individual's success in her endeavors.

> ... merit is not a matter of the objective outcome but of subjective effort. The attempt to achieve a valuable result may be highly meritorious but a complete failure, and full success may be entirely the result of accident and thus without merit. (1960: 95)

Judgment of another's merit (or demerit) requires information about the desires, intentions, efforts, beliefs, and costs of that person's conduct that we rarely, if ever, possess and that the employees at the Department of Merit Assessment will certainly never possess. Moreover, the extraction of much of this information would involve highly intrusive investigations into the particular details of the lives of the citizenry. Furthermore, even if some agency possessed all the information that reasonably might be thought to be indicative of one or another sort of merit (or demerit), that agency is extremely unlikely to have access to a generally acknowledged way of weighing these different sorts of merit (or demerit) to arrive at a broadly accepted merit score for diverse individuals. Thus, it is exceedingly unlikely that dispersals on the basis of the merit points assigned to individuals will be seen to accord with general and impartial norms of desert and the equal treatment of all under the law. Rather, such dispersals will be seen as a matter of officials passing out differential benefits to particular individuals on the basis of their ill-informed predilections about what constitutes personal desert. The Desert is Unknown Argument makes a strong epistemic case against the proposal that some agency equipped with coercive powers should seek to apportion income (or holdings) among the members of society in accordance with their degree of personal desert. The argument is quite general because it does not depend upon desert being understood as painful effort aimed at some beneficial result. Unfortunately, it has the defect of not being an argument against the dominant, end-state type of distributionist principles.

The Desert as Contribution Proposal

In *CL* Hayek suggests a more positive stance concerning justice in holdings than any offered in *MSJ*. This more positive stance turns on "the distinction between value and merit" (1960: 94). "[T]he value which a person's capacities or services have for us and for which he is recompensed has little relation to anything that we can call moral merit or deserts" (1960: 94). In contrast to merit, the value of an economic agent's conduct is a matter of what others are prepared to pay for that conduct or for the goods produced by that conduct. Perhaps justice in income or holdings is a matter of individuals receiving market payment for the goods or services they provide for others. Two premises underlie this proposal. The first is that justice is a matter of receiving remuneration for goods or services in proportion to their contribution to the recipients of those goods and services. The second is that the measure of the contribution of goods or services to their recipients is the payments that those recipients freely agree to make in exchange for those goods or services. In sum, free market payments for the goods or services one provides are just because they are proportionate to the contribution one makes to the recipients of those goods or services.

> It is of the essence of a free society that a man's value and remuneration depend not on a capacity in the abstract but on success in turning it into concrete service which is useful to others who can reciprocate. ... In a free society we are remunerated not for our skill but for using it rightly. (1960: 80–1, 82)

This view can be construed as a type of desert doctrine, that is, desert as contribution. Although an agent may not deserve her talents or even her willingness to engage in painful effort, when she engages those talents or painful (or painless) efforts in a way that contributes to others as measured by their willingness to pay for those contributions, she *deserves those payments*. In fact, Nozick thinks that, in endorsing this view in *CL*, Hayek is unintentionally endorsing a pattern doctrine, viz., "distribution in accordance with the perceived benefits given to others" (1974: 158). Nevertheless, it is at most a *very* atypical pattern view. For there is no central distributor who remunerates individuals in proportion to the extent that they have provided (in Nozick's words) "perceived benefits given to others." As Hayek says in *MSJ*, "The remunerations which the individuals and groups receive in the market are thus determined by what these services are worth to those who receive them ... and not by some fictitious 'value to society'" (1976: 76). This is no societal measure of the value of the contributions of diverse individuals that tells us what contributors should receive instead of the actual market remunerations that they garner.

The Signal Argument

In both *CL* and *MSJ*, Hayek contrasts the ill-effects of attempting to reward individuals for their pain and effort with the benefits of market remuneration for valued economic activities. The basic ill-effect of attempting to reward individuals for their pain and effort is to *encourage* painful effort without regard to the value of the goods or services that these efforts yield. Do we really want a system that provides incentives for engaging in costly *attempts* to provide valued goods or services and penalizes people for finding easier and less painful ways of providing them? However, if the rationale for market remuneration is not to reward pain and penalize avoidance of pain, what then is its rationale?

One view of the rationale for market remuneration is provided by the Desert as Contribution Proposal. Another is that market remuneration functions to encourage the creation of high-valued goods and services and to discourage the allocation of resources to low-valued goods and services. This is the *incentive* rationale for affirming market returns. However, it is not surprising that Hayek is especially attracted to an *informational* rationale. The function of market remuneration is to signal market participants that they are likely to benefit from shifting to certain economic activities (and away from others). When people respond to such signals, human and material resources are reallocated from less valued toward more highly valued uses.

> [T]he functioning of the market order of particular prices or wages, and therefore of the incomes of the different groups and individuals, is not due chiefly to the effects of the prices on all those who receive them, but to the effects of the prices on those for whom they act as signals to change the direction of their efforts. Their function is not so much to reward people for what they *have* done as to tell them what in their own as well as in the general interest they *ought* to do.[17] (1976: 71–2)

Still, economic agents will be alert to such signals and motivated *voluntarily* to shift their efforts toward activities that promise better market returns only if "doing what in fact most benefits others ... will secure the best reward" for those agents – which is to say, only if people are rewarded in accordance with perceived contribution. A regime that, instead, arranges for people to receive in accord with "their individual merits or needs," will have to find some other way to get people to engage in the activities that the regime deems to be most economically beneficial (1976: 72). Note also that within a system that remunerates individuals in accordance with the value that others place on their contributions, and within which remuneration provides individuals with information about what economic activities they should switch to or abandon, the resulting array of income will reflect all sorts of contingencies and will not conform to any end-state or pattern distributionist principle.

The No Authority Argument

Hayek holds that the institution of social justice requires that "the members of society should organize themselves in a manner which makes it possible to assign particular shares of the product of society to the different individuals or groups." As Hayek sees it, this raises the awkward question of "whether there exists a moral duty to submit to a power which can co-ordinate the efforts of the members of society with the aim of achieving a particular pattern or distribution regarded as just" (1976: 64). His suggestion, of course, is that there is no such power with a right to our submission. Unfortunately, Hayek seems here to rely again on his presumption that to advocate social justice is to advocate distribution in proportion to individual (subjective) desert. For, it seems that it is only such a patterned goal that would require a regime with the power to engage in detailed investigation and monitoring and administration of individuals. On the surface at least, a regime that imposes a general tax-and-transfer scheme to fulfill some end-state formula would not need to subject individuals to such investigation, monitoring, and detailed administration.

Two better bases for Hayek's concern about advocacy of social justice undermining spontaneous free society do not depend on his mistaken assumption that advocacy of social justice means advocacy of distribution according to individual merit. The first of these was mentioned within the discussion of the Signal Argument. A really serious commitment to distribution according to merit or needs or (fairly strict) equality would likely involve levels of taxation that would seriously reduce people's incentives to devote themselves (and their economic resources) to high-valued economic activities and, therefore, would likely require at least some shift to a command economy in which individuals are ordered to devote themselves (and their economic resources) to activities deemed socially valuable by those occupying the commanding heights.

> Once ... rewards correspond not to the value which their services have for their fellows, but to the moral merit or desert the persons are deemed to have earned [or even to some egalitarian-leaning end-state principle], they lose the guiding function they have in the market order and would have to be replaced by the commands of the directing authority. (1976: 82)

If brain surgeons are unwilling to bear the stress of a third decade of practice for only three times the average net annual income, they may have to be conscripted into the National Surgical Corps. Unanticipated negative consequences of such interferences – e.g., less people training to be brain surgeons – will typically be interpreted as revealing the necessity of further coercive interventions, for example, requiring people to train as brain surgeons. The second better basis for concern about advocacy of social justice is the way in which such advocacy politicizes society. I label this the Political Dynamic Argument.

The Political Dynamic Argument

According to Hayek, a core feature of the market order – including remuneration on the basis of the value that others place on the goods or services one provides to them – is that it is "a wealth-creating game (and not what game theory calls a zero-sum game) that is, one that leads to an increase of the stream of goods and the prospects of all participants to satisfy their needs" (1976: 115). The institution of the rules of just conduct and the rules by which people make things their own provides the framework for this mutually advantageous order. In contrast, distributionist principles are essentially zero-sum in the sense that their institution requires the ongoing imposition of losses on some individuals (who have never acted contrary to the rules of just conduct) in order to provide gains for other individuals. Quite aside from whether a theoretic case can be made for some determinate distributionist principle, actual advocates of social justice will always disagree among themselves about what the correct principle of social justice is and, consequently, about who should receive assistance in the name of social injustice and who should pay for it.

Once credence is given to the social justice impulse, political life becomes more and more an ever-mutating zero-sum game in which new, self-appointed representatives of newly discovered victims of social injustice are continually contending for inclusion within a coalition that has decent prospects of gaining political power and imposing the costs of that coalition's social justice programs on other members of society.[18] The power of such coalitions is fueled by the degree to which claims about social injustice motivate its members to join one another against their perceived victim-izers. For Hayek, this dynamic involves a reversion to tribalism – a focus on group identity within which group members are taught to think of certain other identity groups as their friends and others as their enemies. For Hayek, the rise of campaigns for social justice is a sign of, and a further cause of, a tribalist revolt against liberal individualist cosmo-politanism (1976: 133–52).

A key effect of the politics of social justice is an increase in government powers which are thought – Hayek believes mistakenly – to serve the real interests of the victims of estab-lished power. To maintain or expand their power, those in office have to at least pretend to cater to the special interests of those who put them in power. They have to validate the worldviews of their supporters – especially the view that the only hope for people encountering difficulties in their lives is an increase in state power that is wielded by political entre-preneurs who really care about them.

It was in the belief that something like "social justice" could thereby be achieved, that people have placed in the hands of government powers which it can now not refuse to employ in order to satisfy the claims of the ever increasing number of special interests who have learnt to employ the open sesame of "social justice". (1976: 67)

The result, according to Hayek, is that,

This greatest triumph of personal freedom the seduction of "social justice" threatens again to take from us. And it will not be long before the holders of the power to enforce "social justice" will entrench themselves in their position by awarding the benefits of "social justice" as the remuneration for the conferment of that power and in order to secure to themselves the support of a praetorian guard which will make it certain that their view of what is "social justice" will prevail. (1976: 99–100)

Possessors of power who are not highly skilled at holding together an electoral praetorian guard will give way to contenders who are better yet at assembling a coalition of the aggrieved.

I want to conclude this chapter by mentioning a few more of Hayek's many noteworthy contentions. One of the ways that a zero sum perspective on the world is built into common patterns of speech is the presumed linkage between one person being "advantaged" and others being "disadvantaged." If, all of a sudden, *A* becomes more intelligent, alert, or physically vigorous than *B* through *Z*, it is said that *A* has become advantaged and that *correlatively B* through *Z* have become disadvantaged. Such an inference from *A*'s advantage to *B* through *Z*'s disadvantage would make sense if these twenty-six individuals were competing for a single prize – that is, if they are engaged in a zero-sum game. But the inference is totally inappropriate if *A* through *Z* are participants in a multi-dimensional market economy.

[T]he acquisition by any member of the community of additional capacities to do things which may be valuable must be regarded as a gain for that community. It is true that particular people may be worse off because of the superior ability of some new competitor in their field; but any such additional ability in the community is likely to benefit the majority. (1960: 88)

If, say, all of a sudden, five of this group of twenty-six individuals become more intelligent, alert, or physically energetic, it is extremely likely that all the other individuals will be net gainers.

It is striking, though, that immediately after making this point about enhanced abilities or opportunities for some not being disadvantageous for others, Hayek anticipates a Nozick-like Lockean proviso. The fact that all are at least likely to gain when some have increased abilities and opportunities,

> implies that the desirability of increasing the abilities and opportunities of any individual does not depend on whether the same can also be done for the others – provided, of course, that others are not thereby deprived of the opportunity of acquiring the same or other abilities which might have been accessible to them had they not been secured by that individual. (1960: 88)

Indeed, Hayek goes well beyond such a proviso by endorsing a tax-funded safety net. Thus, in *CL* he says, "There are good reasons why we should endeavor to use whatever political organizations we have at our disposal to make provision for the weak or infirm or for the victims of unforeseeable disaster" (1960: 101). And in *MSJ* he asserts that "There is no reason why in a free society government should not assure to all protection against severe deprivation in the form of an assured minimum income, or a floor below which nobody need to descend" (1976: 87). It is, though, fair to say that Hayek does not make clear what the good reasons for an assured minimum are.

5
Objections: Internal and External

Introduction

This chapter will focus on objections within and around political libertarianism. By objections "within" libertarianism, I mean disputes among libertarians or among libertarians and their near neighbors along the ideological spectrum. There are, indeed, many such disputes. However, for the purposes of this book, the most important of these disputes concerns the extent of the legitimate or justifiable state – or, more generally, the range of acceptable coercive institutions. By objections "around" libertarianism, I mean philosophical critiques of libertarian doctrine by theorists who are quite distant from libertarianism along the ideological spectrum. There are, indeed, many such attacks – originating from numerous different locations along that spectrum. I will concentrate on attacks that proceed from the dominant intellectual left – from the large and diverse camp of theorists who would describe themselves as "liberal egalitarians" or "egalitarian socialists." I will be able to examine only a small representative sample of such attacks. I will consider briefly Rawls' own critique of libertarianism and then a bit less briefly critiques offered by Liam Murphy and Thomas Nagel and by G. A. Cohen.

Anarchy, the No Taxation Minimal State, and the Taxation Minimal State

The internal libertarian debate about the justifiability of the state – the exemplar of a coercive institution – is itself complex and multi-dimensional. We can, however, examine the key contentions and most interesting objections and responses by considering three contending positions – Free Market Anarchism, the No Taxation Minimal State, and the Taxation Minimal State. We will also take note of two versions of the No Taxation Minimal State position (see Figure 5.1). Important contributors to libertarian theory, for example, Hayek and Lomasky, ultimately endorse a Taxation *Semi-Minimal* State, which both funds its activities through taxation and extends its activities beyond the protection of the rights of life, liberty, and estate. It may extend its tax-funded activities to financing public goods such as scientific research or mosquito abatement; and it may provide a basic safety net – perhaps in the name of a moral right to assistance or on the basis of more pragmatic considerations.[1] Putting aside the classical liberal Semi-Minimal State, we will focus here on three alternative libertarian institutional proposals.

We can most readily explain the positions shown in Figure 5.1 and engage the contentions, objections, and responses among advocates of these positions in terms of the persons' first-order Lockean rights of life, liberty, and estate and their second-order Lockean rights to engage in self-defense, the enforcement of restitution for rights violations, and the infliction of punishment for rights violations.[2] The libertarian view that emerges from taking these rights very seriously – as Nozick does in *ASU* and as do his free market anarchist opponents – is that coercion is justifiable if and only if it is directed against rights-violating conduct. Each person's rights to life, liberty, and estate entail her rights against the coercive violation of those rights. And each person's rights to defense, restitution, and retribution entail her rights to use and authorize coercion against violations of her first-order rights of life, liberty, and estate. No one has a right not to be subjected to the coercive suppression or nullification of the effects of her rights-violating coercion. To what conclusion

Free Market Anarchism ↔ No Taxation Minimal State ↔ Taxation Minimal State

Competing protection agencies; network provision of rights-protective law to voluntary, subscribing clients (plus free riders)	Single monopoly (unified, "federal" network); provision of rights-protective law to voluntary, subscribing clients (plus free riders)	Single monopoly (unified, "federal" network); provision of rights-protective law to taxed subjects

Nozickian
Monopolistic
Enterprise

Constitutionally
Constrained
Political Structure

Figure 5.1 Free Market Anarchism, No Taxation Minimal State and Taxation Minimal State

about the nature and scope of justifiable coercive *institutions* do these libertarian claims about the rights of individuals lead?

The standard and most readily understandable libertarian answer to this question is the No Taxation Minimal (or "night-watchman") State – the NTMS. It is an essential feature of *any* state that it engages in – or stands ready to engage in – coercion. Advocates of the NTMS generally maintain that it is unique among states in its compliance with libertarian principles because it employs coercion only to enforce reasonable articulations of people's basic rights to life, liberty, property, and contract – and only in ways that do not themselves violate rights. It limits – or seems to limit – its use of force or the threat of force to coercive defensive action, coercive implementation of restitution for rights violations, and coercive infliction of punishment for rights violations. Most strikingly, the NTMS does not finance its operations through the coercive extraction of funds, that is, taxation, from those whose rights it purports to protect. Rather, the NTMS finances its operations through the sale of its protective services to willing buyers of those services.

But, here is a complication. As any *state* must, NTMS claims for itself a monopoly on what it takes to be the legitimate use of coercion within the territory or over the population it rules and it must at least somewhat successfully enforce that monopoly. As a state, the NTMS does not allow significant challenges to its being the final authorizer of coercive force within its realm.[3] Note, though, that the enforcement of such a monopoly itself involves the *coercive* suppression or control of would-be alternative suppliers of legitimate defensive, restitutive, and retributive services. So, as Nozick recognized in *ASU*, the key question for the vindication of the NTMS is whether the coercion that the NTMS employs to sustain its monopoly on defensive, restitutive, and retributive services is itself permissible coercion. Nozick's elaborate defense of the NTMS in *ASU* is fundamentally an argument for the permissibility of the coercion that the NTMS must employ to maintain its position as the monopoly supplier (or authorizer) of coercive protective services.

In contrast to advocates of the NTMS, some libertarians, for example the economist Ludwig von Mises[4] – who was Hayek's more libertarian mentor – advocate a taxation-funded minimal state, the TMS. Such advocacy may be defended by arguing that, if adequate funding of protective services will not be available through voluntary subscription, taxing people to finance such activities is a necessary evil. Or, perhaps, under those circumstances, such coercive takings do not count as rights violations. We need to keep this later possibility in mind as we move through this section's discussion. Both the NTMS and the TMS eschew the employment of coercion to enforce morality (beyond the morality of respect for others' rights) or to suppress voluntary, self-harming actions. Coercive moralistic or paternalistic interventions are as unacceptable as coercive redistributive interventions. Decent human beings will be disturbed by various sorts of immoral or self-harming activities and may seek in non-coercive ways to discourage them (Mill 1978 [1859]). Nevertheless, to sanction the state's coercive suppression of vice or self-injury is to invite every group with contentious ideas about what constitutes vice or self-injury to battle for state power to enforce its disputatious ideas or to block the enforcement of other groups' contentious doctrines. It is to invite the demise of liberal pluralist society. Note also that the same limits on coercive state action apply to the state's conduct toward foreign agencies – be they states or non-state organizations. The only justification for a minimal state's action against such agents is the protection of the rights of its own citizens or clients through measures that are not themselves rights-violating. (Exactly what coercive defensive measures against attackers count as morally permissible is, of course, another disputed issue within libertarianism.)

The most prominent defender of free market anarchism (hereafter, FMA) during the time that Hayek was writing his major works in political theory, and Nozick was transitioning from democratic socialism to libertarianism was the economist, Murray Rothbard. And, indeed, Nozick tells us that his interest in vindicating the NTMS arose from rights-based critiques of the minimal state that he encountered in conversations with Rothbard[5] (1974: xv; Raico 2002). The FMA's broad-brush critique of the state is that the state is the greatest mass-murdering, enslaving, brutalizing, depreciating, and subordinating institution in human history. It is organized predatory force, which typically asserts some special religious or moral authority that purports to sanctify its activities – activities that would immediately be perceived as criminal in the absence of some sanctifying theology or ideology (Rothbard 1974). The state is the fundamental and well-honed device through which we human beings seek to fulfill our natural desire to live at the expense of others. As the mid-nineteenth-century French laissez-faire economist, Frederic Bastiat put it, "The state is the great fiction by which everyone endeavors to live at the expense of everyone else" (Bastiat 2012 [1848]: 97). In reality, the state generates a Hobbesian struggle in which we (our group or coalition) seek to capture the coercive mechanisms of the state and to use it against others before they capture it and use its powers against us. Since it is the essence of the state to be an instrument for killing and predation, should a more constrained state come into existence – e.g., the NTMS or the TNS – it will fairly quickly revert to the more murderous and exploitative mean. For, the anarchist reasons, there can be no sustained reliable checks on the coercive powers of any *monopoly* state.

The FMA's *moral* charge against the TMS is that it sins twice against individual rights. It sins by coercively extracting from its peaceful subjects the funds that it purports to devote to the protection of their rights. And it sins against individuals and associations who seek to compete with the TMS in the provision of protective services by forbidding them from offering such services. Even the NTMS is guilty of the second of these sins. FMA's *economic* charge against both sorts of minimal state is that the monopoly provision of any service is certain to yield shoddier, less fine-tuned, less innovative, and more expensive forms of that service than would be supplied by a competitive market. Only a competitive market for valued services – including protective services – will efficiently allocate economic resources to the diverse services that people demand. (Recall the argument against central planning discussed in Chapter 3.) Advocates of minimal monopoly states forget the lessons of their own pro-market *economic* arguments. The FMA's *social theory* charge against both sorts of minimal state is that they presume that an apt and desirable legal order must be the deliberate product of – the promulgation of – the state. However, legal order need not arise from state promulgation. Hayek – himself no advocate of a market in protective services – insists that legal order arises prior to and independently of the state (1973: 72–4).

Nozick agrees with free market anarchists that no state authority has ever been established by any actual social contract and that it is most unlikely that there ever will be a social contract that will establish state authority.[6] He reminds us that the "tacit consent," which is often invoked by social contract theorists, "isn't worth the paper it's not written on" (1974: 287). Therefore, Nozick seeks to provide a vindication of the NTMS that does invoke anything like a social contract that is designed to yield a state. Rather, he seeks to vindicate the NTMS by indicating how it would – in invisible-hand fashion – arise from a state of nature through the permissible actions of individuals and their associations. He seeks to show how, starting from the very circumstances and types of rights-protective adaptations and agencies envisioned by the advocate of FMA, the NTMS would arise through entirely permissible actions and transactions.[7]

According to both the free market anarchist and Nozick, a Lockean state of nature is not the horror that a Hobbesian state of nature is. Most occupants of a Lockean state of nature have some appreciation of the rights of others as equal and independent beings and some disposition as rational beings to abide by those rights. We can attribute to most of those individuals a disposition toward reciprocal respect for each other's life, liberty, estate, and contractual claims on the basis of a Humean–Hayekian (and Lomaskian and Schmidtzian) story about people's perception of the benefits of such reciprocal respect and about the selection over time of social orders that are more fit for survival and imitation because they embody and reinforce such norms.[8] Nevertheless, according to the free market anarchist and Nozick, this state-less condition is not a walk in the park. Deliberate violations of rights will still take place as will honest disputes among good-willed parties about what their property and contractual rights and obligations are. Individuals who act as judges in their own cases are likely to be biased on their own behalf in their understanding of the relevant norms and relevant facts; and they are likely to be believed to be biased. Even individuals who appeal to the appropriate norms and have their facts right may well lack the force to carry out their proper defensive, restitutive, or retributive actions – in part because others will not know whether they should be trusted. Whereas Locke presumed that these inconveniences could only be overcome by the intentional creation of political society and the state, Nozick and the free market anarchist maintain that one must investigate whether individuals have the moral and intellectual resources to overcome these inconveniences without the resort – or at least intentional resort – to the state (1974: 11).

Markets provide what people demand.[9] Good-willed individuals in the state of nature would seek out and find enterprising protection agencies which would offer them the service of *reliable* rights protection. Reliable rights protection for a client requires that her protection agency will have entered into agreements with other good-willed agencies about how precisely they will construe the rights of their potential customers. How precisely will the boundaries between various types of physical property be determined? What precisely must be in a contract to support the claim of a given contractual obligation? These codifications will not be plucked out of thin air but, rather, will likely embody evolved norms that articulate and protect property and contractual rights. Through such specifications – subject to clarifications and extensions as they are called for by changing circumstances and discoveries – positive law is restated and developed. To the extent that protective agencies wisely do not attempt to deal with all possible disputes in advance, they will seek to insure reliable and peaceful resolutions by establishing or subscribing to arbitration agencies – that is, judicial enterprises – that will supply judgments in the cases brought before them.

Rogue protective agencies that do not abide by the judgments of their selected judicial counsels or that select only biased counsels will not be able to provide their clients with reliable and peaceful dispute resolution. For the endeavors of those agencies will not be honored by non-rogue agencies. The decisions of judicial enterprises which are subscribed to by non-rogue agencies will further refine the norms that individuals will have reason to expect will be complied with or enforced. Coalitions of non-rogue protective agencies will suppress outlaw agencies that may seek to violate the increasingly well-defined rights of the clients of those protective agencies. At the same time, the various agencies will compete with one another for customers on the basis of price, quality of service, and specialized expertise. Some agencies may specialize in protection against industrial espionage, others against violations of royalty agreements for natural gas extraction; some arbitration agencies may specialize in disputes concerning industrial espionage, others in disputes concerning royalty agreements. Advocates of such a competitive system for the private provision of law maintain that it would provide better products at lower costs than any state monopoly; a system of competing private providers is as likely to work better than a state monopoly in the rights-protection arena as in, say, the provision of groceries, clothing, and housing.

Subscription to a protection agency will at least normally involve an agreement to eschew private acts of defense, restitution, and retribution. For protective agencies will not want to be drawn into – and to be known to be susceptible to being drawn into – conflicts on the basis of their clients' freelance coercive activities. (Protective agencies may refuse to network with other agencies that allow their clients to engage in private defense, restitution, and retribution.) And subscription to a protection agency will at least normally involve agreement to pay for services rendered. Thus, within a system of competing protective agencies, protective services are not financed through impermissible coercive extraction of funds from the clients of those agencies.

The scenario offered by the free market anarchist ends with this projection of a network of competing protective agencies. However, Nozick adds two phases to this scenario which together complete his invisible-hand account of the NTMS. In the first of these further phases, one of the protective agencies or the cooperative network as a whole seems to attain a *natural* (non-coerced) monopoly in the provision of protective services. Nozick holds that *natural* monopolies are rare because the creation of a monopoly normally requires illicit coercive suppression of competition. Thus, he has to ask, "Why is this market different from all other markets?" (1974: 17). His answer is that conflict resolution will be simplest and least costly when both parties to a dispute subscribe to the same agency. So, for any given individual, settlement of disputes will be simplest and least costly if she subscribes to the protective agency with the most clients. Hence, the higher the percentage of the population that becomes customers of a given agency, the greater the competitive advantage that agency possesses over its rivals. "[S]ince the worth of the less than maximal product declines disproportionately with the number who purchase the maximal product, customers will not stably settle for the lesser good, and competing companies are caught in a declining spiral" (1974: 17).

Nevertheless, it is not clear how decisive this factor would be. The fact that it may be less complicated and costly to resolve automobile collision claims when both parties are customers of the same insurance company has not lead to one company having a virtual monopoly within the automobile insurance business. In addition, Nozick's argument seems to overestimate the homogeneity of the services that competing protective agencies would offer. As FMA advocate Roy Childs put it, "An infinite variety of institutions can develop in society, concerned with as many different aspects of protection" (2007: 222). It may well be that prospective clients will care more about the specialized protections offered by diverse agencies than being a client of the agency with the most clients. Moreover, as Rothbard points out

(2007: 234), Nozick moves awfully quickly from competing agencies agreeing upon procedures to resolve disputes between them to there being "one unified federal judicial system" (1974: 16). Still, we should note Tyler Cowen's much more ingenious argument for the non-coercive transformation of a cooperative network of competing protective agencies into something like a monopoly state (or cartel of agencies). According to Cowen, precisely to the extent that competing protective agencies would create a complex grid of common rules, dispute resolution mechanisms, judicial procedures, and so on, those agencies will be able effectively and *non-coercively* to preclude further agencies from entering into competition with them. All the already networked agencies need do is to refuse to allow those further agencies to integrate into the established grid (Cowen 2007).

In any case, it is crucial to see that Nozick's case for the NTMS does not really rest on the claim that such a monopoly in protective services would arise through *non-coercive* market processes. According to Nozick, non-coercive processes would yield only a "dominant protective association" – a DPA. Scattered among the clients of this DPA, there still would be independent self-enforcers of rights and niche providers of protective services who are not correctly classified as "outlaws." The DPA may not simply suppress these independent and niche *non-outlaw* providers. Yet, according to Nozick, the non-outlaw, protective activities of these independents and niche providers have to be monitored, regulated, or channeled by the DPA for that institution to qualify as a state. How, though, can a DPA *permissibly* coerce non-outlaw competitors to submit to its guidance? This brings us to the second and crucial phase which completes Nozick's invisible-hand account of the permissible formation of the NTMS. Within this phase the DPA permissibly attains statehood through its permissible *coercive* interference with those remaining non-outlaw self-protectors and competing protective services.

Nozick's implicit premise here is that independent self-protectors and sellers of protective services – who have declined to submit to the DPA strictures about what procedures need to be followed for reliably ascribing guilt or liability for rights violations and for justly engaging in restitutive and retributive responses – pose a significant risk of violating the rights of the DPA's clients.[10] Nevertheless, these self-enforcers and outlier providers of protective services are not outlaws. *Thus, they pose too little risk to justify simple prohibition of their activities. On the other hand, they pose too much risk for those clients of the DPA simply to have to tolerate.* Fortunately, according to Nozick's explicit premise, there is a middle path between allowing non outlaw, but risky, private or outlier enforcers to proceed at will and simply suppressing them (Nozick 1974: 83). That middle path is to interfere, to forbid, or re-channel those private or outlier risky activities while also duly compensating those subject to such interference. The formulation of this middle path that delineates permissible interference with risk-posing, but non-outlaw, protective agents is Nozick's "Principle of Compensation," according to which "those who are disadvantaged by being forbidden to do actions that only might harm others must be compensated for these disadvantages foisted upon them in order to provide security for others" (1974: 82–3). Given this "Principle of Compensation," a DPA may demand that aspiring self-protectors and outlier agencies conform their protective activities to the standards and practices established by it as long as the DPA offers due compensation to the proscribed agents. The DPA's exercise of this oversight authority over otherwise somewhat risky freelance rights-enforcers makes it an "ultra-minimal state" which finances itself through the sale of its services to parties who are free not to purchase those services from it (or its approved auxiliaries) but, then, would have to go without protective services. Nozick says that due compensation for those who are disadvantaged by being forbidden to carry out their somewhat risky protective activities would likely take the form of their receiving the state's protective services for free or at a reduced rate. In Nozick's terminology, when, as a matter of due compensation, the ultra-minimal state extends protective services to some individuals free of charge or at a discounted rate, it becomes a minimal state.

Roy Childs objects that the compensation that is to be offered to individuals who, because of their principled opposition to the monopoly state seek to be self-enforcers of their rights will consist in being brought under the protective umbrella of a monopoly state. "What is he willing to give us as compensation for being so prohibited? He is generous to a fault. He will give us nothing less than *the State*" (2007: 223). However, this objection misses the mark. According to Nozick, parties who are forbidden to be self-protectors may receive compensation in kind or in cash. "The prohibitor must completely supply enough, in money or in kind, to overcome disadvantages" (1974: 112). And recipients of monetary compensation "may, of course, refuse to pay the fee [for the state's protective services] and so do without these compensatory services" (1974: 113). The real issue is whether the Principle of Compensation is plausible. If it is plausible that moderately risky private rights enforcement is subject to proscription as long as the proscribed party is duly compensated, then a frustrated self-protector who is offered due compensation, cannot complain that he is being treated unjustly on the grounds that, despite the riskiness to others, he *wants* to be a freelance enforcer of his rights. Rothbard does criticize the Principle of Compensation by saying that, according to it, one is "permitted to cavalierly invade someone's home and break his furniture, simply because [one is] prepared to 'compensate' him afterward" (2007: 240). However, this criticism ignores Nozick's complex discussion of the special conditions that need to be present for one to be permitted to "boundary cross" even if one makes due compensation.[11]

Childs offers a different and more powerful criticism of Nozick's NTMS, viz., that once it comes into existence, there are no detectible checks on its power. After all – see the lower left part of Figure 5.1 – that state is an entirely non-political institution. It is simply a monopolistic enterprise owned by its shareholders and normally controlled by its board of directors and senior management.

> There is no question of a constitution, of course, merely the contracts with its clients, which in the case of conflicts it alone can judge and interpret. There is no voting. There is no separation of powers, no checks and balances, and no longer any market checks and balances either. ... What happens in the event of its assuming more power? Since it is a monopoly, any disputes over its functions are solved exclusively by itself. (2007: 224)

In a nice twist, Childs maintains that we have more reason to be concerned about the *risk* of the DPA achieving monopolistic statehood through its subordination of self-enforcers and outlier protective agencies than we have to be concerned about the risks posed by those parties (2007: 224). Even if the NTMS does not turn to rights-violating predation, for example taxation, if the members of the network that constitute the NTMS do form an effective cartel and are thereby able to attain long-term monopolistic pricing for their increasingly shoddy services, the provision of those services will no longer have the virtues that the *pro-market* advocate of the NTMS expects it to have. On the other hand, if the members of the network remain sufficiently in competition with one another so that the characteristic defects of monopoly provision do not arise, then it will be far from clear that the network has become a *state*.

Free market anarchists maintain that the only credible check on the activity of any protective agency is the existence of competing agencies to which individuals may turn when that first agency goes rogue. Still, a possible alternative to market checks on rights-protective enterprises is political-constitutional constraints on the NTMS. A DPA that aspires to being a monopolist provider of rights-protection might *self-impose* such constraints in order to show that its transition to monopoly provider is not as risky to individuals at large as are the risky self-enforcers and niche agencies which the dominant agency moves to suppress or oversee. From a libertarian perspective, such constitutional constraints and procedural requirements would have to impose clearer, stricter, and more effective limits on the scope of acceptable state action than, say, the original US Constitution imposed. In her novel, *Atlas Shrugged*, NTMS advocate Ayn Rand has Judge Narragansett, one of her minor heroes, adding a clause to the US Constitution that forbids state abridgement of freedom of production and trade (1957: 1083). Hayek himself went from celebrating the US Constitution for its success at limiting state power (1960: 176–92) to declaring it to be a failure (1973: 1) and to proposing an alternative, more resiliently liberty-protective constitutional structure (1979: 105–27).

We must, however, return to Nozick's question, "Why is this market [in rights-protective services] different from all other markets?" For, there is a very different, widely accepted answer to this question that poses a considerable difficulty for both the advocate of the NTMS and FMA. This answer is that the anticipated product of this market, viz., rights-protection, is (largely) a *public good*. For our confined purposes here, we can think of a public good as a good which, if it is produced and enjoyed by some members of a given public, cannot readily be withheld from other members of that public. The standard and useful example of a public good is national-scale defense. For the sake of simplicity, imagine a defensive shield that would protect everyone within a large region against any aggressive attack from outside of that region. Imagine further that the shield is genuinely a *good*; its benefits clearly exceed its costs. Indeed, for each prospective consumer of that shield, there is a range of monetary payments that this individual would gladly make in order to gain the benefit to her of this good *were she not able to gain that benefit without paying for it*. Now imagine that an agency – perhaps an NTMS or perhaps a private construction firm – sets out to market the production of this shield. And imagine that this agency knows the prices that each prospective consumer of the shield would gladly pay to attain the protection of the shield *were she not able to gain that benefit without paying for it*.

Not appreciating the significance of this last italicized clause – but, instead, expecting a healthy profit – the state or firm sets out to take orders for the provision of the shield. The conventional economic wisdom (which *might* be mistaken) is that the total value of the orders that the state or firm will receive will be markedly less than it naively expects. Indeed, the total value of the orders may easily be less than the costs of producing the shield. The explanation, of course, is that each prospective consumer may reason that: (i) the likelihood of the shield being produced will not be significantly affected by whether or not she places an order for it; (ii) if the shield is produced, she will get the benefits of it whether or not she places an order; and (iii) she gets to retain the proposed payment if and only if she declines to place the order. On this basis, each prospective consumer may decline to place an order for the defensive shield with the hope of free-riding on its being financed by the orders of others who have not reasoned so cleverly. The problem with people reasoning in this way is not that some people will succeed at being free-riders but, rather, that no one will get to be a free-rider or even a paying-rider because the voluntary financing scheme will fail due to the number of individuals who seek a free-ride.

The lesson that is conventionally drawn from such considerations is that any public good will be at least significantly under-funded unless the prospective consumers of that good are taxed to pay for it. Such taxation prevents those consumers from being too clever for their own good. *If* one accepts this conclusion with respect to the public good of national-scale defense and extends it to the more complicated case of the intra-societal protection of rights[12] – and one ought not to rush to these judgments – advocates of both FMA and the NTMS will be in a decidedly awkward position. For their honoring of people's rights by eschewing taxation will require that they forego offering an effective defense of those rights.

To escape the awkwardness of endorsing institutions in the name of rights which, to honor those rights, will not effectively protect them, libertarians may have to swallow the bitter pill of the TMS, which seems to render itself capable of effectively protecting rights by dishonoring them, that is, by coercively extracting from individuals the funds it needs to protect people against coercive infringements. Perhaps, however, that pill is not so philosophically bitter. For, perhaps by introducing a bit of complexity into our understanding of people's rights,[13] it can be argued that *this* coercive extraction is morally permissible. Person's rights indicate what must not be done to them – or more specifically, what must not be done to them without their consent. But what about cases in which consent is not feasible? As Nozick says after summarizing the reasons for always prohibiting boundary crossings that are not consensual, "The complication is that some factor may prevent obtaining this prior consent or make it impossible to do so" (1974: 71). A person's right over her own body entails that she has a right not to be cut open without her consent even by an expert surgeon seeking to save her life. However, what if the person who needs that surgery to save her life is already unconscious and, hence, unable to give consent? If it is permissible for the surgeon to proceed with the needed surgery on the already unconscious individual, this seems to be true because the requirement that the subject consent to the physical intervention is really a requirement that she consent if and only if consent is feasible.

So, the libertarian advocate of the TMS may argue that, precisely because of the non-feasibility of attaining consent from individuals to make payments in exchange for the public good of rights-protection, it is *permissible* to impose those payments without actual consent. Hence, although a TMS finances itself through coercion, it does not do so through impermissible, rights-violating coercion. Recall, however, that this defense of the TMS turns on a striking assumption about information. It assumes that the state's tax assessors would know, for each assessed party, what magnitude of taxation would leave that party net better off in light of the value for that party of her receipt of the tax-funded public good of protective services.[14]

Rawls' Critique of Libertarianism

John Rawls' most extended critique of libertarianism appears in his *Political Liberalism* within a section devoted to defending his view that the primary concern of a theory of justice must be the specification of a society's just basic institutional structure (1993: 262–85). Rawls' core complaint against libertarianism is that it recognizes no special role for, and thus denies a need for, such a basic structure (1993: 262). A libertarian might counter this claim by saying that libertarianism endorses a basic legal structure that articulates and enforces Nozickian historical entitlement principles or Hayekian rules of just conduct. However, Rawls denies that this is what he has in mind as a basic structure. Instead, Rawls envisions an institutional structure through which deep features of the *Rawlsian* program – especially the achievement of fairness and the overcoming of moral arbitrariness – would be advanced. Of course, the libertarian might respond by saying that it is not much of a criticism of libertarianism to point that it fails to endorse an institutional structure that is devoted to ends that the libertarian disavows. Moreover, from a libertarian perspective, the thesis that a core role of political and legal institutions is to nullify in the name of fairness whatever is said to be morally arbitrary is deeply mistaken. I do not intend here to arbitrate this dispute. Rather, my goal is to show that Rawls' own account of what the basic structure would do – or what its operators would do through it – strongly *supports* the refined version of Nozick's "How Liberty Upsets Patterns" argument that I develop in Chapter 4 (see pages 84–7). That argument, it will be recalled, is directed against the ongoing application of any pattern or end-state doctrine of distributive justice.

Here is a brief restatement of that argument which focuses more specifically on the operation of a Rawlsian basic structure. The social engineers who operate the levers of the Rawlsian basic structure will lay down rules of acquisition and policies of taxation and transfer that are expected to result in an array of incomes that satisfies the difference principle. Persons will have legitimate expectations that the incomes they have attained through activities that have been entirely in accord with the rules and policies promulgated by the basic structure will be secured for them in the name of justice. For Rawls, to *deserve* a given income is simply to have such a legitimate expectation of receiving it under the operation of the rules and policies enacted by the basic structure (1971: 310–15).

The problem is that, without violating the rules and policies laid down by the basic structure, enterprising individuals will deploy the resources assigned to them in the name of justice in unilaterally and reciprocally advantageous ways that (as Hayek would predict) are not anticipated by the social engineers. And the resulting array of enhanced (or undiminished) incomes will almost certainly be (or be seen to be) unjust from the perspective of the basic structure that is devoted to the difference principle. For, the enactment of a redesigned package of rules and policies by that basic structure will convert (or will seem to convert) this unanticipated array of enhanced (or undiminished) incomes into one that more fully satisfies the difference principle. The basic structure must continually make such adjustments in society's governing rules and policies in order to keep it honed in on distributive justice. However, such adjustments in the rules of the game must defeat at least some of the legitimate expectations generated under the antecedently proclaimed rules and policies. Furthermore, each subsequently adjusted (non-Stalinist) package of rules and policies will leave room for another round of unanticipated enhanced *and legitimately expected* incomes some of which will, nevertheless, have to be redistributed through further adjustments in the basic structure. In short, the basic structure's ongoing mission of insuring outcomes that accord with the basic distributionist principles of justice requires the ongoing defeat of legitimate expectations of individuals who have conducted themselves entirely in accord with the rules and policies that have been enacted for the sake of satisfying those principles. If the reliable honoring of people's legitimate expectations is essential to justice, Rawls' activist basic structure is antithetical to justice.

Rawls obviously has this Nozickian criticism in mind when in *Political Liberalism*'s chapter on the basic structure he tells us that within the social and economic regime that he advocates,

> There are no unannounced and unpredictable interferences with citizens' expectations and acquisitions. Entitlements are earned and honored as the public system of rules declares. Taxes and restrictions are all in principle foreseeable, and holdings are acquired on the known condition that certain transfers and redistributions will be made. The objection that the difference principle enjoins continuous corrections of particular distributions and capricious interferences with private transactions is based on a misunderstanding.[15] (1993: 283)

Rawls' response, then, is to say that there will be no unexpected adjustments, there will be no interferences with and no contravention of legitimate expectations. Taxes and restrictions are all ("in principle") foreseeable and (Rawls' language suggests) any transfers or redistributions of acquired holdings are similarly anticipated. Thus, whatever legitimate expectations arise will be fulfilled. The problem for Rawls is that this response is systematically contradicted by Rawls' own account of the proper and necessary role of the basic structure.

According to Rawls, a basic structure is needed to create and maintain the fair background conditions that must obtain if the outcomes of apparently just modes of inter-action are to be actually just. "[T]he distribution resulting from voluntary market transactions ... is not, in general, fair unless the antecedent distribution of income and wealth, as well as the structure of the system of markets, is fair" (1993: 266). All the parties to the interactions must have enjoyed fair equality of opportunity, there must be no inequality of economic circumstances among the transacting parties that gives one party an unfair bargaining advantage, and so on. "The role of the institutions that belong to the basic structure is to secure just background conditions against which the actions of individuals and associations take place" (1993: 266). The outcome of individual activities that fully accord with the rules and policies set forth by the basic structure may in unanticipated ways undermine fair equality of oppor-tunity or create opportunities for taking unfair advantage. The basic structure must block such departures from fairness by modifying the rules and policies it promulgates.

Rawls' account of the need for an activist basic structure emphasizes in almost Hayekian fashion the inability of the operators of that structure to design rules and policies, compliance with which will have the effects that the basic structure is supposed to achieve. "There are no feasible rules that it is practicable to require economic agents to follow in their day-to-day transactions that can prevent these undesirable consequences [of undermining background justice]" (1993: 266). Rawls' claim is not limited to a system of rules that libertarians would endorse.

> The fact that everyone with reason believes that they are acting fairly and scrupulously honoring the norms governing agreements is not sufficient to preserve background justice. ... But, to the contrary, the tendency is rather for the background justice to be eroded even when individuals act fairly: the overall result of separate and independent transactions is away from and not toward background justice. (1993: 267)

> [E]ven if everyone acts fairly as defined by the rules that it is both reasonable and practicable to impose on individuals, the upshot of many separate transactions will eventually undermine background justice. (1993: 284)

All this leads to the judgment that,

> The need for a structural ideal to specify constraints and *to guide adjustments* does not depend upon injustice [i.e., people acting contrary to the promulgated rules]. Even with strict compliance with all reasonable and practical rules, such adjustments are *continually* required. ... A conception of justice must specify the requisite principles and point to the overall direction of political action. In the absence of such an ideal form for background institutions, there is no rational basis for *continually* adjusting the social process so as to preserve background justice, nor for eliminating existing injustice. (1993: 284–5, emphasis added)

The main point here, of course, is that Rawls supports his contention that it is a deep defect of libertarianism that it does not acknowledge the special role that must be played by the basic structure by emphasizing the need for a basic structure that intervenes "continually" to nullify outcomes that arise from people acting in accord with the rules and policies that this structure has itself enacted.

Yet this supports the Nozickian charge that the ongoing pursuit of distributive justice will require continual (periodic) interference with people's possession and discretionary control over holdings to which they have legitimate expectations on the basis of the rules and policies promulgated in the name of justice. The only possible complication here is that Rawls repeatedly says that the continual intervention by the operators of the basic structure is for the sake of restoring "background justice." So, perhaps Rawls is saying that an activist basic structure is needed only to deal with unanticipated deviations from background *fairness*[16] – unanticipated undermining of fair equality of opportunity – that arise even when people act within the rules and policies enacted by the basic structure. This complication would only require a slight modification in the Nozickian charge cited above, viz., the substitution of "fairness" for "distributive justice."

Moreover, Rawls may also be acknowledging – as he should – that continual interference will be needed to nullify arrays of income that arise from people acting in accord with the promulgated rules and policies because those distributions do not best satisfy the difference principle. Surely, if the results of people engaging in economic interactions that fully accord with the promulgated rules and policies will tend to undermine fair opportunity and for this reason will require interference by the basic structure, then those interactions will also tend to yield distributions of income that are unjust in the sense of not best satisfying the difference principle and will likewise require interference by the basic structure. Rawls' recognition that an activist basic structure will also be needed for the sake of satisfying the difference principle (and not just fair equality of opportunity) seems to be indicated in the last sentence from Rawls cited above. There Rawls says that "In the absence of such an ideal form for background institutions, there is no rational basis for continually adjusting the social process so as to preserve background justice, *nor for eliminating existing injustice*" (1993: 285, emphasis added). These existing injustices, which arise under the auspices of the already functioning "social process," would seem to be unforeseen incomes attained by individuals acting within the rules and policies enacted by the basic structure – incomes that must to some degree be nullified because of their distributional unacceptability.

Rawls cannot have it both ways. He cannot assert both: (i) that libertarianism is defective because it does not acknowledge the need for a constantly vigilant basic structure that continually changes the rules and policies to maintain fairness or justice in income distribution; and (ii) that the Nozickian "How Patterns Upset Liberty" critique is mistaken because under the auspices of a Rawlsian basic structure, "There are no unannounced and unpredictable interferences with citizens' expectations and acquisitions" (1993: 283).

Murphy and Nagel on the Illusions and Confusions of Libertarianism

One main purpose of Liam Murphy and Thomas Nagel's *The Myth of Ownership* (M&N 2002) is to explain why the appeal of libertarianism – especially the appeal of its invocation of property rights in its complaints about taxes – is based on illusion and confusion. According to M&N, the appeal of libertarianism arises from people's failure to appreciate the significance of property rights being creatures of legal conventions and of property rights being made possible by tax-funded state action. Their core message takes a leaf from the book of Rousseau. Property rights are not the bounty of nature but, rather, they are the gift of the state; and when in its wisdom the state reorganizes or redistributes property, individuals can have no complaint based on natural moral rights. Stated more fully, "a dominant theme" of their discussion is:

> Private property is a legal convention, defined in part by the tax system; therefore, the tax system cannot be evaluated by looking at its impact on private property, conceived as something that has independent existence and validity. Taxes must be evaluated as part of the overall system of property rights that they help to create. Justice or injustice in taxation can only mean justice or injustice in the system of property rights and entitlements that result from a particular tax regime. (2002: 8)

M&N say that private property is a matter of convention and that private property is made possible by the state and its tax system. It is not entirely clear what the division of labor is between these two claims. Perhaps it is something like this: First, since private property is a matter of legal convention (which M&N *automatically* construe as state-established convention), private property has no "independent existence and validity." Private holdings would have independent existence and validity if they were reflective of natural rights. However, they cannot be reflective of natural rights because they are entirely creatures of convention. Second, taxes are necessary to fund the legal conventions that establish and enforce property rights; and taxes also support a range of entitlements to goods and services provided by the state. What is subject to assessment is the whole complex of existing private holdings, taxes, and entitlements. A variety of moral considerations may enter into this assessment. However, it is illicit to appeal to natural rights considerations even in the assessment of the system as a whole.

Perhaps, natural rights considerations are excluded because M&N implicitly hold to the Benthamite view that all rights are merely matters of actually existing legal or moral conventions. "Most conventions, if they are sufficient entrenched, acquire the appearance of natural norms; their conventionality becomes invisible" (2002: 9). The appearance that natural norms are embodied within or manifested by the conventions is always mere appearance. Aside from legal conventions definitive of legal rights, M&N mention societal conventions governing different roles for men and women. And they then declare, "it is essential, in evaluating [conventions], to avoid the mistake of offering as a justification precisely those ostensibly 'natural' rights or norms that are in fact just the psychological effects of internalizing the convention itself" (2002: 9). M&N offer belief in extra-legal property rights as their prime example of a belief that is simply "an unreflective sense of what are in fact conventionally defined property rights." This lack of reflection gives "... rise to an even more confused criticism of the existing system on the ground that it violates natural property rights, when, in fact, these 'natural' rights are merely misperceptions of the legal consequences of the [conventional] system itself" (2002: 9). According to M&N, "the instinctive sense of unqualified ownership has remarkable tenacity" (2002: 35). However, this never suggests to them that anything other than confusion and illusion might lie behind this "instinctive sense."

As far as I can see, M&N never offer parallel debunking analyses of norms that *they* want to appeal to in their assessments of existing systems. They never say,

> Here are conventions that seem to embody or manifest norms of equality or fairness or benevolence; but one must avoid the

mistake of appealing to equality or fairness or benevolence as justifications for these conventions. For our attachments to equality or fairness or benevolence are in fact the psychological effects of internalizing those conventions.

Nor do they ever say that appeals to the extra-legal ("natural") rights that they wish to invoke, for example, rights of "freedom of expression, freedom of religion, freedom of association" and so on (2002: 64) are "merely misperceptions of the legal consequences of the [conventional] system itself." For M&N, it is entirely sensible to oppose a restriction of speech by invoking a *moral right* to free speech that is the justification for existing or proposed legal conventions that are protective of speech, while it is unreflective confusion to oppose a restriction on someone's use of her property by invoking a moral right to property that is the justification for existing or proposed legal conventions that are protective of property. The result is a ban on appeals to any sort of natural rights arguments in the assessment of positive law governing property, contract, or taxation. M&N are comfortable with this ban partly because they construe any appeal to natural rights of property as bare, *foundationless* assertions. Any such appeal simply takes such rights "... as given, and neither in need of justification nor subject to critical evaluation" (2002: 8). I hope that one lesson of this book is that libertarian theorists – including those who cast their arguments in the language of natural rights – do not take property rights "as given, and neither in need of justification nor subject to critical evaluation."

M&N do offer a rationale for distinguishing between "the basic personal rights: freedom of expression, freedom of religion, freedom of association" and so on (2002: 64) and rights to enter into voluntary economic contracts and to retain the fruits of one's labor. Their claim is that the former rights are included within the "... degree of sovereignty over themselves [that individuals retain] even when they are members of a collective social order" (2002: 64) while the latter rights are not. For, M&N maintain, the choices or activities that are protected by "basic personal rights" are "at the core of the self" (2002: 66), while the choices and activities protected by the economic rights are not. However, this claim is deeply problematic. This affirmation of basic personal rights runs counter to M&N's general skepticism about extra-legal rights. If, despite that skepticism, M&N affirm extra-legal rights of expression, religion, and association, we need an explanation for why *these* affirmations are not merely errors that arise from our familiarity with conventional protections of freedom of expression, religion, and association. By and large, existing positive law still is more strictly protective of freedom of expression, religion, and association than it is protective of freedom to do as one sees fit with one's labor, talents, and property. So, given M&N's belief about our disposition erroneously to infer extra-legal rights when we encounter conventional rights, shouldn't we be *more* suspicious of extra-legal personal rights than extra-legal economic rights? M&N perceive interferences with one's "right to speak one's mind, to practice one's religion, or to act on one's sexual inclinations" (2002: 65) as markedly more crucial to human autonomy than the grubby freedom to operate a food truck despite the city council machinations of restaurant owners to forbid competition, or to sell oranges one has grown to willing buyers without the constraints imposed by a state marketing board. But perhaps the autonomy that is crucial to some people is not the autonomy that is crucial to others. Nevertheless, to their credit, M&N do articulate the libertarian objection to their selective affirmation of rights.

> The state has no more right to demand a cut of the profits for redistribution in exchange for its maintenance of the peaceful conditions of cooperation than it would have to demand adherence to a particular religion for the same reason. To champion other liberal rights while belittling economic freedom is morally inconsistent. That is the libertarian position. (2002: 66)

And, then, M&N offer no rebuttal to this challenge. They simply say that, "we are out of sympathy with it" (2002: 66).

M&N's core argument seems to turn on the proposition that, if the state articulates and enforces rules that enable people to enjoy certain property rights, taxes and regulates that property in various ways, provides diverse goods or services to property holders and others, and those property holders are better off than they would be without the state, then those propertied individuals cannot claim that the taxes and regulations imposed on them by that state are unjust. (For M&N, it is really easy for the state to render everyone better off since the alternative to the state is the Hobbesian state of nature.) Here's one (fictional) example that brings out the implausibility of M&N's key proposition. Recall the original (1960) version of the movie, *The Magnificent Seven*. Calvera (played by Eli Wallach) and his band of banditos have been preying upon a village of peaceful Mexican farmers for years. Some of the villagers convince Chris Adams (played by Yul Brynner) to recruit a band of out-of-work good guys to protect the village against the banditos in exchange for food and lodging. (However, let us ignore this contract as we should ignore any claim that the state is created by a social contract.) The banditos attack; but they are driven off by Brynner and his six colleagues. But, now envision a philosophical epilogue to the movie in which Adams finds and reads *The Myth of Ownership*.

Enlightened by this work, Adams announces that he and his heroic colleagues will be constituting themselves as a state and as this state they will be sticking around to protect the village against subsequent bandito predation; and he and his colleagues will only extract from the villagers 85% of what the banditos have extracted. He explains to the somewhat stunned villagers that, while there may be some sort of moral considerations that speak against the system under which they will now live, they can have no complaint against the system on the basis of their rights to their pre-tax income. To dramatize his stance, Adams orders that the following explanation from *The Myth of Ownership* (2002: 32–3) be painted on the wall of the village barn – merely substituting "safety from banditos" for "markets" and adding an appropriate parenthetical clarification:

> There is no safety from banditos without government and no government without taxes. ... It is therefore logically impossible that people should have any kind of entitlement to all (*or any of*) their pretax income.

M&N's main argument seems to make no essential use of their repeated assertion that property rights are the creatures of conventions and, therefore, can have no "independent existence and validity." However, it is easy to construct an argument that centers on this assertion and fits comfortably within M&N's overall perspective. The value of considering such an argument is that the libertarian response to it involves a nice fusion of the Lockean–Nozickian and Humean–Hayekian strands within libertarian theory. The anti-libertarian argument is that libertarian theorists purport to have insights about people's basic natural rights or about the principles, compliance with which make peaceful and mutually beneficial social order possible. Yet the abstract principles that libertarian theorists purport to discover and prize lack connection to and relevance for the vast array of much more concrete rules on which actual peaceful co-existence and cooperation to mutual advantage depend. According to this anti-libertarian argument, these abstract principles are at best pie in the sky, while the really fruitful stuff is the array of much more specific conventional rules by which we navigate our interactions with one another. M&N might argue that, since those more fine-grained conventional rules do the work of specifying people's actual rights, it makes no sense to invoke those abstract natural rights in assessing those rules; nor do those abstract natural rights play any proper role in assessing the legal rights created by those conventional rules. The conventional legal rules say that I have a right to that portion of my income that those rules allow me to retain – until those rules are changed. According to M&N, a moral assessment of the whole system of rules and its consequences is possible; but not on the basis of those pie in the sky natural rights.

At the core of this sort of reasoning is the presumption that, if natural rights theorizing is to be relevant to the assessment of actual, real-life, concrete rules, that theorizing *itself* must deliver affirmations or denials of those concrete rules. According to this presumption, if I assert that I have justly acquired a certain five-acre patch of previously unowned land by driving forty stakes with my name on them along the boundary lines of those five acres, natural rights theory can only support my claim by providing a philosophical proof that driving in forty such stakes is the morally valid way to acquire five acres of previously unowned land.

Since it is silly to think that natural rights theorizing can provide such a proof, the conclusion is reached that, *ceteris paribus*, whether driving in the forty stakes creates a right to those five acres is purely a matter of convention.

However, just about every advocate of natural rights (or principles of natural justice) rejects this presumption and, instead, offers a picture in which there is a division of labor between assertions of natural or basic rights (or principles of natural justice) and convention. The main contentions of such advocates are:

i) Abstract natural or basic rights or principles of justice limit the sets of more fine-grained rules that are morally eligible for adoption. (For instance, the conventional rules governing property within the regime established by Chris Adams would violate the peasants' abstract natural right to the fruits of their labors.)

ii) Abstract natural or basic rights or principles of justice do not dictate a single set of more fine-grained rules that must be adopted in the name of those rights or principles. There are many imaginable sets of more fine-grained rules that are eligible for adoption as articulations of those abstract natural or basic rights or principles of justice.

iii) If a morally eligible set of usefully fine-grained rules does come into existence – whether through pure historical contingencies, through a Hayekian evolution of norms, or through Nozickian-minded CEOs – a key basis for respecting those rules will be their instantiation of otherwise merely abstractly stated moral rights or principles of justice.

iv) A further basis for reciprocal compliance with any set of morally eligible and fine-grained rules that we might be lucky enough to find in operation is that such compliance enables those rules to do what they are supposed to do, viz., facilitate rights-respecting and mutually beneficial interaction among us. Nozick himself makes a parallel point about how a particular location becomes "the place to go" for teenagers in pursuit of company. It does not become the place to go by being the eligible place that philosophical reasoning identifies as the place to go. Rather, it becomes the place to go because "others benefit from, and count upon, your converging upon that place, and similarly you benefit from, and count upon, their congregating there" (1974: 140). Similarly, a set of eligible fine-grained rules become the rules to comply with by being a set of such rules that we are apt to converge upon.

Locke understood the need for the concretization of otherwise merely abstract laws of nature and the fact that those laws of nature nevertheless remain the basis for compliance with the acceptable concretizations when he wrote,

> The obligations of the law of nature cease not in society, but only in many cases are drawn closer, and have by human laws known penalties annexed to them, to inforce their obser-vance. Thus the law of nature stands as an eternal rule to all men, legislators as well as others. (1980: §135)

Such a view is common among more recent libertarian authors who are within or close to the natural rights camp. Nozick himself points out that it would be an error to think that natural rights constitute "some set of principles obvious enough to be accepted by all men of good will, precise enough to give unambiguous guidance in particular situa-tions, clear enough so that all will realize its dictates, and complete enough to cover all problems that will actually arise" (1974: 141). Rasmussen and Den Uyl deny that philo-sophical reasoning can identify some best set of fine-grained property rules. Instead, there is a considerable range of eligible sets of rules any one of which would satisfy the telos of property rights (2005: 103). The vagueness of fundamental principles is remedied by contingencies that present them to us in more fine-grained form. Thus, Lomasky maintains that "The basic liberty right to acquire and use property is made concrete through the social recognition of conventions that define which actions constitute appropriation and transfer of property" (1987: 123). For an extensive development of the idea that the natural and abstract right of property is a right to others' compliance with whatever set of more fine-grained and largely conventional rules actually serve to define for a society a coherent practice of property, see Mack (2010).[17]

G. A. Cohen's Anti-Capitalist Egalitarianism

G. A. Cohen was probably the most talented philosophical defender of egalitarian socialism writing in the several decades after the publication of Nozick's *ASU* and Hayek's *LLL*. Cohen takes Nozick's most basic contentions to be that each individual has pre-political moral rights over herself and to the fruits of her labor. Liberal egalitarians like Rawls and Nagel readily and confidently reject natural rights forms of libertarianism precisely because these basic contentions had no traction for them. In contrast, Cohen saw that his own Marxist socialism was (or at least seemed to be) implicitly founded on these very contentions. Capitalism was to be condemned because it is based upon depriving workers of the fruits of their labor to which they have just claims in virtue of their rights over themselves and their labor. Only under socialism will the workers enjoy the full fruits of their labor. Thus, Cohen felt that he had to confront and defeat Nozick – preferably without having to deny their shared premises – in order to maintain his own (increasingly less Marxist) commitment to socialism.

The result was a series of powerful critiques of *ASU* which formed the basis of Cohen's *Self-Ownership, Freedom, and Equality* (Cohen 1995). In that work, Cohen runs through a series of attacks on the doctrine of *ASU*. He attacks Nozick on initial acquisition and on the thesis that just transformations from just situations must yield just outcomes (1995: 19–66), and on the adequacy of Nozick's Lockean proviso (1995: 67–90). Finally, he directly confronts self-ownership and argues that it too must be rejected (1995: 229–44) precisely because of the *truth* of the libertarian claim that, if persons do have basic moral rights over themselves, they also have rights to the usually unequal fruits of their respective labor (1995: 213–23). However, an exposition and critical examination of *Self-Ownership, Freedom, and Equality* is beyond the scope of this book.[18] Instead, here I shall consider Cohen's short book, *Why Not Socialism?* (Cohen 2009), which was his final attempt to express persuasively his deeply egalitarian and socialist convictions. This will allow us to focus on some important general issues rather than to dwell on specifically Nozickian stances. We will see how Cohen sought to remain more egalitarian and more anti-capitalist than ordinary liberal egalitarians – while, at the same time, more fully embracing the need for market mechanisms!

Why Not Socialism? introduces us to the charms of the camping trip – which is presented as the antithesis of life within a market economy. We see the attractions of this respite from our ordinary capitalist lives of buying and selling and crassly looking after number one. As Cohen depicts it, the camping trip is a bit of egalitarian socialist paradise. All the resources available for the trip are treated as common property. There is none of the repugnant bargaining and haggling that is endemic to market-based societies. Whatever needs to be done on the trip gets done more or less spontaneously because of everyone's devotion to everyone else's equal enjoyment. According to Cohen, the camping trip stands in radically sharp contrast to life in a market society which is deeply imbued with fear and greed.

> [T]he market motivates productive contribution not on the basis of commitment to one's fellow human beings and a desire to serve them while being served *by* them, but on the basis of cash reward. The immediate motive to productive activity in market society is (not always but) typically some mixture of greed and fear ... [T]he market posture is greedy and fearful in that one's opposite-number marketeers are predominantly seen as possible sources of enrichment, and as threats to one's success. (2009: 39–40)

It seems that it would be marvelous if the ethos of the camping trip could replace the ethos of market society (as Cohen depicts it) as the basis for ongoing, large-scale social order.

According to Cohen, the camping trip realizes and enhances our appreciation for two principles: the principle of socialist equality of opportunity and the principle of community. The former holds that justice requires equality of enjoyment. However, since enjoyment is not so easily titrated, in practice it calls for equality of income. The basic case for this principle is the now familiar and essentially Rawlsian argument that: (i) since no one deserves their nature or nurture, no one can have any just claim to any differences in enjoyment (or income) that arise from her nature or nurture; (ii) since almost all differences in enjoyment (or income) arise from differences among people's nature or nurture, almost all such differences are not just; (iii) since almost all such differences in enjoyment (or income) are *not just*, almost all those differences are *unjust* and justice, therefore, requires their elimination. "When socialist equality of opportunity prevails, differences in outcome reflect nothing but differences of taste and choice, not differences in natural and social capacities and powers" (2009: 18).

Cohen offers no general statement of the principle of community. Instead, he describes two different aspects of this principle. One aspect is the value of *being in community* with others. According to Cohen, the rich individual who usually drives her expensive car to work cannot be in community with the working stiffs who regularly ride the bus to work. When the rich individual rides the bus one day because her car is in the shop, she cannot *commune with* the regular riders about how uncomfortable the ride is. Not surprisingly, for Cohen, the fundamental obstacle to being in community with others is inequality of income. "We cannot enjoy full community, you and I, if you make, and keep, say, ten times as much money as I do, because my life will then labor under challenges that you will never face" (2009: 35). Substantial inequality of income leads to some people being regular bus passengers and to other people being drivers of (or being driven in) luxury cars. Such inequalities of income need to be eliminated for the sake of community.

This appeal to community enables Cohen to be more egalitarian than liberal egalitarians who subscribe to "luck egalitarianism." Luck egalitarians say that the reason that differential outcomes that result from the natural and social lotteries are unjust and must be negated is that these lotteries are not entered into voluntarily. In contrast, if an individual does voluntarily buy a regular lottery ticket (or engages in some other voluntary gamble) and wins, that increment to her income is not unjust; and, if she loses, that deduction from her income is not unjust. So, according to luck egalitarianism, it will *not* be just to seize the winnings of a voluntary lottery player even if she intends to buy a luxury car with them, and justice does not demand redress for those who do not win. Cohen agrees with luck egalitarians that the inequalities that arise from voluntary gambling "are not condemned by justice." Nevertheless, "they are repugnant to socialists when they obtain on a sufficient scale, because they contradict community" (2009: 34); and, thus, they must be annulled.

The second aspect of community that Cohen presents involves a contrast between "market reciprocity" and "communal reciprocity." "If I am a marketer, then I am willing to serve, but only in order to be served: I would not serve if doing so were not a means to get service" (2009: 41–2). In contrast, in communal reciprocity,

> what I want, as a non-marketeer, is that we serve each other ... To be sure, I serve you in the expectation that (if you are able to) you will also serve me. My commitment to socialist community does not require me to be a sucker ... I nevertheless find value in both parts of the conjunction – I serve you and you serve me.[19] (2009: 43)

According to Cohen, "A nonmarket cooperator relishes cooperation itself" whereas the market cooperator "does not value cooperation with others for its own sake" (2009: 42).

Let us consider whether it is feasible for a large-scale, ongoing society to be governed by the ethos that Cohen believes to govern the camping trip. One crucial problem is that the camping trip is about 99.6 percent consumption activity. All the gear, all the food likely to be consumed, all the first aid equipment, all the maps, and so on are just there – like manna from heaven. There are no problems of production to be solved on the camping trip. Yet a camping trip can be a respite from the task of solving such problems only because those problems are solved within the larger ongoing society. Cohen is at least implicitly aware of this. For, when he turns to the feasibility question, he focuses on how production might be effectively organized in a non-capitalist society. Strikingly, his first observation is that problems of production will not be solved by socialist central planning. For he has come to accept the fundamental contention of Mises and Hayek that the only way to have a rational allocation of resources to valued ends is to have genuine market prices for those resources and ends. Nevertheless, this does not lead Cohen to abandon all hope for a society that is socialist, at least in the sense of being radically egalitarian and being populated by people who are not mere marketeers.

Cohen pins his hopes largely on a scheme developed by Joseph Carens (1981). Carens notes that, within a capitalist system, market prices have both an informational and a motivational function.[20] Within his scheme, market prices are supposed to fulfill their informational function but not what Cohen takes to be their repugnant motivational function. Within Carens' proposal, individuals and firms will act like marketeers seeking to buy low and sell high and will take their cue for their profit- and wage-maximizing conduct from the signals provided by the resulting market prices. CEOs will aggressively maximize profits – because this maximizes the value of what is produced over the cost of producing it. Investors will maximize profits – because this moves capital toward its most productive uses. Workers will pursue the highest available return for their labor – because this moves labor to its most economically valued employment. And so on. The result will be capitalist economic efficiency but without the horrors of fearful and greedy marketeer motivation. For, everyone's motivation behind this show of capitalist selfishness will be the enhancement of societal income for the sake of its equal division. On tax-and-transfer[21] day, those who have garnered more than equal incomes will attain their underlying egalitarian purpose by surrendering their surplus income, while those who have fallen short will receive their equalizing recompense. As Cohen sees it, the deeply anti-capitalist egalitarian can appropriate the capitalist social technology of market prices for egalitarian purposes. All that is necessary is a substantial – albeit not total – transformation of human motivation. As J. S. Mill presciently put it, the proposal is to carry on "the whole round of the operations of social life without the motive power which has always hitherto worked the social machinery" (2006: 737).

Here we can note only some serious weak points within Cohen's final challenge to the libertarian vision of a society of diverse individuals with commitments and purposes of their own who are, nevertheless, able to live at peace with one another to mutual advantage by respecting one another's basic rights as they have taken more fine-grained form. Let us start with Cohen's picture of life on camping trips and his picture of life within (non-Carensian) market societies. There are camping trips and camping trips and Cohen does not tell us much about the one he envisions. It sounds like it involves a score or so people who seem to know one another in advance and voluntarily join in the trip in part because of their knowledge of their trip partners. Trips of that size, for example multiple day rafting trips, often are organized by commercial outfitters. The core equipment – rafts, cooking gear, chemical toilets – belong to the outfitter while individuals bring their own tents, sleeping bags, cameras, hiking gear, and so on. On such commercial trips, the rafting guides have a good deal of authority about, for example, what campsites to stop at and which particular hikes to do along the way. I have never seen anyone feel oppressed by this type of authority, nor feel that the relationship between the guides and the customers was one of cold mutual exploitation. But let us put aside guided commercial trips. People engage in self-organized rafting or kayaking or backpacking trips that may include as many as fifteen or so – although that's an awfully big size for a backpacking venture. These almost always involve friends or friends of friends or people who are vouched for by friends. People bring their own gear and, although no one spends time putting "Private Property" stickers on their gear, the gear is definitely not treated as public property to be used for the sake of equal enjoyment. Neither collective life nor equal enjoyment motivates people on the trip. Contrary to Cohen, no one goes on a camping trip with the goal of relaxing "on condition that she contributes appropriately to her capacities to the flourishing and relaxing of others" (2009: 4–5).

People are on the trip to enjoy the excitement of the whitewater, the beauty of the surroundings, the challenge of the hikes – all leavened with just the right degree of effort and danger. People enjoy all these things *and* they enjoy being with others who are enjoying these things; and the others enjoy people enjoying their enjoyment. Each person's enjoyment is experienced as a confirmation of each other person's enjoyment. When campers say to one another – as they frequently do – "what a great view, what an exciting stretch of whitewater," they are not conveying information about their surroundings that otherwise would be unnoticed. Rather, they are saying, "I know you too find this beautiful or exciting and I know that you are pleased that I too find it beautiful or exciting." There is a deeply valuable type of community here. But it has nothing to do with collective control of resources or the belief that everyone on the trip is or should be aiming at equality of enjoyment. Everyone – well, almost everyone – is *delighted* when someone has an even more wonderful time than everyone else. They are delighted in the wonderfulness and they don't begrudge the difference.

What about Cohen's picture of life within a (non-Carensian) market order? Interestingly, Cohen does not depict huge corporations crushing little guys. Cohen locates the repugnance of (non-Carensian) market interaction in the much more homey exchanges between the butcher, the baker, and the candlestick maker. The core of Cohen's depiction of market exchange is expressed when he says, "the market posture is greedy and fearful in that one's opposite-number marketeers are predominantly seen as possible sources of enrichment, and as threats to one's success" (2009: 40). Of course, market participants see their trading partners as sources of enrichment. They see prospective trading partners as sources of opportunity, not as enemies. But Cohen's addition of "and as threats to one's success" summons up a view of market exchange that Cohen himself knows to be false, viz., that market exchange is zero-sum; either I enrich myself by threatening the success of the party I transact with or that party enriches herself by undercutting my success. Ordinarily Cohen acknowledges that each trading party wants the other to gain; each wants the other to see a benefit for herself in the exchange (that exceeds her cost) and thereby be induced to enter the exchange. But Cohen takes it to be awful that the benefit provided to his trading partner is not the marketeer's *ultimate* purpose. Indeed, Cohen's thought seems to be that, since that benefit is not the marketeer's ultimate purpose, the marketeer does not *at all* aim at benefiting his trading partner. Yet that aim is real enough to guide the marketeer toward the production of goods or services that will be valued by his intended customers. Moreover, I think many butchers, bakers, and candlestick makers do care about producing and offering goods that are worthy of being desired by their customers. Perhaps they have only acquired this concern because it's good policy; but, again that does not mean that the concern is not real.

In addition, and contrary to Cohen, it is entirely open to marketeers to relish market cooperation, that is, to have both an abstract appreciation for the trading relationship of people giving and receiving value for value and a personal enjoyment in participating in such relationships. Furthermore, Cohen treats market interactions as though they are nakedly self-interested encounters rather than deeply rule-governed activities. Market society is utterly dependent on the general expectation of (almost) all of its members of (almost) everyone's reciprocal compliance with the Humean–Hayekian norms that make cooperation to mutual advantage possible. Although marketeers largely strive to attain their own personal ends, the moral ecology that makes successful striving likely obtains only because of their mutual internalization of the rules of just conduct. Market society operates through and because of *trust*.

We need not pause to examine Cohen's principle of socialist equality of opportunity except to note that it is not a principle of equality of opportunity but, rather, of equality of outcome. However, we must attend a bit to Cohen's much more distinctive principle of community. Cohen's notion of community is flawed in two important ways. The first is his presumption that community requires at least rough equality. Community among individuals requires that each sees himself as belonging to or being a non-eliminable part of the same social association. Perhaps that association involves a basic similarity of roles, like being daily bus riders. But, very often, that community will be tiered and distinctly non-egalitarian. Think of the community that sometimes exists for members of all sorts of hierarchical religious, fraternal, academic, athletic, or commercial associations. Conservative writers may be correct when they assert that community is more readily realized in traditional and hierarchical social structures than in new-molded egalitarian structures. The second is Cohen's presumption that, if the value of being in community is to be realized for everyone, everyone has to be in community with everyone else. But why can't bus riders attain the value of community by being in community with other bus riders while luxury car owners attain the value of community by being in community with other luxury car owners (who get together to grumble about the cost of repairs)? An individual who does not have the good of sociality in her life needs something with much more particular content than becoming a member of the universal community. And part of that more particular content may well be defining herself in contrast to members of some other non-universal community. "We are mountain bikers, not road bikers." "We pray to the real God."

Finally, let's turn to what seems to be Cohen's best hope, viz., the socioeconomic scheme proposed by Carens. How are we supposed to understand the motivation of the individuals functioning within this regime? Presumably they are not moved by actual greed and fear. For, if they are, their daily lives will be the horrible lives of all those trapped within a repugnant capitalist order. In addition, if participants in the scheme genuinely expect equalization at the end of the tax year, it is hard to see how during the year they could be motivated by actual greed and fear. Why get excited about a prospective gain if you know it is going to be dissipated or be fearful of a particular loss if you know it is going to be redressed? So, it seems that participants in the scheme will have to spend their economic lives *mimicking* the lives of people who, on the participants' own theory, live horrible, greedy, and fearful lives. Yet it is doubtful that the participants could pull off this mimicry. It is difficult to see how people who reject the motivational structure that Cohen ascribes to marketeers will be able to figure out how people with that motivational structure would act and will be able to get themselves to act in those ways.

Even if these participants do manage to conduct themselves as though they are marketeers and manage on tax-and-transfer day to equalize the proceeds of their mock capitalist order, it seems they must forego the all-inclusive community that is a crucial value for Cohen. An advanced market order will call for significant role and status differentiation. CEOs have to be driven to work in their Mercedes-Benzes – so they can conduct conference calls and not be subject to the contingencies of bus travel. Managers have to manage and employees must to some extent be managed – and hired and fired. Surely this would be a major barrier to all persons being in community with one another. In addition, the reciprocity within people's transactions would be ugly market reciprocity in which I serve you only (it is said) in order to get you to serve me rather than the beautiful non-instrumental reciprocity in which I serve you for the sake of serving you while you reciprocate in kind. The more successfully participants in the scheme conduct themselves as marketeers, the more they cut themselves off from the type of community that Cohen takes to distinguish his position from mere liberal egalitarianism.

What is, perhaps, most disturbing from a libertarian perspective about Cohen's proposal to appropriate the market social technology is that it proposes to utilize that technology while rejecting that technology's crucial function and virtue. That function and virtue is to enable people *with their own distinct and separate systems of ends* to engage in mutually beneficial cooperative interaction. The prospect of market reciprocity explains why people with deeply different ultimate values need not be enemies but, instead, can live at peace with one another to their mutual advantage. That prospect shows that people do not have to be remolded into devotees of some common "higher" end in order to live well with one another. It shows how a deeply pluralistic and tolerant social order is feasible. Hayek especially emphasizes the significance of

> the discovery that men can live together in peace and mutually benefiting each other without agreeing on the particular aims which they severally pursue. ... [This discovery] made it possible to extend the order of peace beyond the small groups pursuing the same ends, because it enabled each individual to gain from the skill and knowledge of others whom he need not even know and whose aims could be wholly different from his own. (1976: 109)

Although some trading partners may also become friends with shared ends, to recognize the great value of the market's function is to recognize that, for any real flesh-and-blood individual who retains her separate life-defining goals, projects, and commitments, the circle of friendship and love will extend to only a tiny percentage of the human beings who may enter into the circle of her direct or indirect trading partners. The crucial move is the conversion of prospective enemies, whom one must defeat or subordinate to advance one's good, to prospective trading partners with whom one can enjoy mutually beneficial cooperation.

For many political theorists like Cohen, this is not enough because the fundamental goal of political inquiry is taken to be the identification and articulation of a supreme common good – or hierarchy of goods – to which everyone is supposed to be devoted. For such theorists, any coordination that is not coordination for the sake of such a common purpose is denigrated as selfish, conflictual, and "predatory" (2009: 82). However, from a libertarian perspective, a social order that protects each individual's freedom to pursue her own conception of a valuable life through voluntary interaction and community with other equally free individuals is not merely an accommodation to human nature; it is the due recognition of the separate importance of each of us.

Notes

Chapter 1: Introduction

1   The view this book focuses on is often mislabeled, "right-liber-tarianism." This label ignores this view's radical anti-statism, including its rejection of state-enforced moralism and pater-nalism, coercive state action on behalf of special interests, and state diplomatic and military adventurism.

2   These solutions are not limited to standard private property or profit-maximizing institutions. On voluntary mutual aid associations, see Beito (2000). On voluntary communal property arrangements, see Ostrom (1990).

3   Some versions of the mutual advantage approach are couched in "contractarian" terminology. For a libertarian version of such an approach, see Narveson (1988: 2017). Other versions of the mutual advantage approach are couched in "public reason" terminology. For a classical liberal-leaning version of such an approach, see Gaus (2012). See also Vallier (2017).

4   For example, the individualist anarchist Benjamin Tucker defended a species of libertarianism on the basis of Stirnerite egoism (Tucker 1972), while British idealist Bernard Bosanquet defended a species of libertarianism on the basis of his metaphysical socialism (Bosanquet 2001).

Chapter 2: Philosophical Antecedents

1   Although Locke favors the extension of religious toleration to Muslims and Jews, he draws the line at Catholics and Atheists because (he says) they are untrustworthy as citizens.
2   Smith adds, "Nobody but a beggar chuses to depend chiefly upon the benevolence of his fellow-citizens" (1981 [1776]: 27).
3   Smith is more willing than Hume to invoke natural rights. For instance, "The property which every man has in his own labour, as it is the original foundation of all other property, so it is the most sacred and inviolable" (1981 [1776], 138).
4   See Barnett (2004), pp. 192–205.
5   See excerpts from Bentham's *Anarchical Fallacies* in Waldron (1987).
6   Mill also wants to confine the authority of public opinion.
7   See Chapter XI, "Of the Grounds and Limits of the Laisser-Faire or Non-Interference Principle" (Mill 2006 [1848]: 936–71).
8   Contrary to Hume and Smith, Mill seems to think that cooperation does require unity of purpose (1978 [1859]: 41–2).
9   In the preface to the 1864 edition, Spencer repudiates "such teleological implications as are contained in the chapter on 'The Divine Idea'" (1970 [1851]: xii).
10 However, wouldn't society, the monopoly owner of all land, be able to extract in rent almost all of any tenant's product? Also, wouldn't society be able to require all tenants to accept various *non-pecuniary* demands, for example that they subscribe to its dominant religion?

Chapter 3: Libertarian Foundations

1   See Nagel (1981).
2   The Nozickian doctrines discussed in this chapter and the next are covered in more detail in Mack (2014).
3   The rationality of the parties in the original position consists in the fact that "each tries as best he can to advance his interests" (1971: 142).
4   Rawls also refers to it as "the principle of rational prudence" (1971: 29).
5   Or, as Hillel Steiner says, "compossible" (Steiner 1977).
6   Which specific principles (if any) would be agreed to by all rational individuals will depend on the characterization of the

original bargaining position. Surely, then, one must not favor a particular characterization of the original position simply because it yields agreement on the principles one antecedently favors. Yet Rawls tells us that "We want to define the original position so that we get the desired solution" (1971: 141).

7 Rawls says that "a rational man would not accept a basic structure merely because it maximizes the algebraic sum of advantages irrespective of its permanent effects on his own basic rights and interests" (1971: 14). However, a broader conclusion would seem appropriate, viz., a rational man would not accept a basic structure that advances *any* enshrined social end irrespective of its permanent effects on his own basic rights and interests.

8 Hayek's doctorate degrees from the University of Vienna were for Law (1921) and Political Science (1923).

9 For outstanding discussions of Hayek's lifelong intellectual program, see Gaus (2015) and Gaus (2017).

10 On Hayek's defenses of freedom, see Mack (2017).

11 It was partly Nozick's reading of Mises and Hayek that moved him from democratic socialism to libertarianism.

12 The planned construction of this bridge *with the resources that are to be devoted to this project* will be part of a rational economic order if and only if these resources would not better serve other more worthy projects. How is the central planner to know whether this is the case?

13 To some degree central planners can make semi-rational resource allocation decisions by mimicking the price-based allocations within market societies.

14 See the essays on Socialist Calculation in Hayek (1948).

15 It is commonly argued that pure private property/market regimes will under-allocate resources to the production of public goods. I take up this issue only within my examination of Nozick's case against individualist anarchism in Chapter 5.

16 Hayek emphasizes the informational role of prices almost to the exclusion of their motivational role. However, the mere belief that one can combine a number of low value resources into a product whose value exceeds the value of its components will not move one to carry out that combination. Typically, one will be *moved* by the prospect of capturing at least a portion of the enhancement in value. "A price is a signal wrapped up in an incentive" (Cowen and Tabarrok 2015: 84). Also see Tabarrok (2015).

17 Even within *designed* social orders, the recognition that subordinates may have important local information favors allowing

them to exercise some discretion in carrying out their assigned tasks.

18 Libertarians often note the inconsistency of those who seem to understand and celebrate spontaneous ecological order while having no comprehension of spontaneous economic order.

19 Recall Locke's view that freedom consists in others not infringing upon one's "person, actions, possessions, and [one's] whole property" (1980 [1689]: §57).

20 This epigraph for Hayek (1976) is from Lippmann (1937: 267).

21 See the sections on "Schmidtz's Pluralist and Indirect Consequentialist Theory of Justice" (pp. 27–36) and "Consequentialism and Strict Enough Compliance" (pp. 36–8) in the online chapter.

22 See Mack (2006b).

Chapter 4: Economic Justice and Property Rights

1 The analogy is not perfect. Unlike a competitive game, all the agents within a market economy can be winners.

2 There are special problems concerning the rectification of injustices done in the distant past. Nozick once mentioned to me his suspicion that injustices have something like a half-life; their demands diminish over time. Perhaps the point is really epistemic. Our access to evidence needed to justify forcible rectification diminishes over time. See "Those Who Cannot Forget the Past are Doomed to Repeat It" in Schmidtz (2006: 213–15).

3 In another departure from taking seriously the separateness and distinctness of persons, Rawls attends to distributions among *representative* persons.

4 The numbers within the matrices represent absolute, not relative, purchasing power.

5 See "the Tale of the Slave" (1974: 290–2).

6 Instead of simply refusing to let *G* and *H* leave, a clever regime might allow them to ransom themselves through payments to the Department of Redistribution.

7 Rawls says, "By contrast, the government's authority cannot be evaded except by leaving the territory over which it governs, and not always then" (1993: 222).

8 Also see Mack (1995).

9 See the last paragraph of this chapter for *Hayek's* opportunity proviso.

10 See note * at (1974: 178–9).

11 Individuals are justifiably "made to obey" certain rules when "although it would be in the interest of each to disregard them, the overall order on which the success of their actions depends will arise only if these rules are generally followed" (Hayek 1973: 45).

12 Recall that, if anything is the ultimate end for Hayek, it is the abstract "order of actions" that arises (in some concrete form) when these rules of just conduct are observed. See Hayek (1976: 16–17).

13 Recall Locke's contention that freedom consists in the non-violation of one's rights of life, liberty, and estate (1980 [1689]: §57).

14 Hayek sometimes does include the procedures that establish ownership among the rules of just conduct. For instance, "*The rules of just conduct* thus delimit protected domains not by directly assigning particular things to particular persons, but *by making it possible to derive from ascertainable facts to whom particular things belong*" (1976: 37, emphasis added).

15 Rawls takes it to be a virtue of his end-state difference principle that it rescues us from "meritocratic society" (1971: 106–7).

16 Here Hayek forgets the extent to which socialists favored central planning simply because it was taken to be scientific.

17 See also Hayek (1976: 115–17).

18 Of course, people who mistakenly describe themselves as victims of *social* injustice may well be the victims of *actual* injustice.

Chapter 5: Objections: Internal and External

1 Recall from the online chapter Lomasky's endorsement of a right to basic assistance (pp. 20–1) and the discussion of "Another Route to a Safety Net" (pp. 38–9).

2 Whether retributive punishment is justifiable is itself a contentious issue among libertarians.

3 See Hayek (1960: 425, note 30) for references to the contention that a monopoly on the use of force is an essential feature of the state.

4 I thank David Gordon and Steve Horwitz for the example.

5 Apparently Rothbard himself had earlier been converted from utilitarianism to the natural rights approach by the most prominent non-academic defender of the NTMS at the time, Ayn Rand (1964a: 1964b). On this conversion, see Childs (1994: 271).

6 For the classic individualist anarchist critique of such a social contract, see Spooner (1973 [1870]).

7 Why does Nozick think that showing that an NTMS *would* emerge *were* people to act rationally and permissibly establishes the legitimacy of any *actual* NTMS that may arise? The best discussion of this question is found in Bader (2017).

8 Experimental economists and game theorists have always found individuals to be more rule-compliant than simple individual utility maximizers would be. See Axelrod (1985) and Bicchieri (2005).

9 For the sort of account that follows, see Tannehill and Tannehill (1972), Friedman (1973), and Rothbard (1973, 1978).

10 So, at least one way of getting evidence that a self-protector or outlier protective agency poses too much risk to have to be tolerated would be to see if that party would decline to accept membership in the network. Contrast this with Cowen's story about how the network can become a state by denying membership to potential competitors!

11 See Mack (2014: section 2.4).

12 Both a networked association and an NT-minimal state may decline to send its police to protect a non-subscriber and may exclude a non-subscriber from its courts. However, the provision of defensive and juridical services *to its subscribers* may less directly have enormous benefits – enormous positive externalities – for the non-subscriber. Hence, the public good dimension of *intra-societal* rights-protection.

13 Much more complex versions of these thoughts are examined in Mack (2011).

14 The advocate of the TMS will have to explain why the state would not be justified in taxing to finance other sorts of public goods.

15 To be fair, we should note that Nozick's objection is to "continuous corrections of particular [legitimately expected] distributions." He does not accuse the distributionist of favoring "capricious interference with private transactions."

16 In this chapter in *Political Liberalism*, Rawls seems to treat "justice" and "fairness" as synonyms.

17 Also see Mack (2015) and Bryan (2017).

18 For an extensive examination and critique see Mack (2002a, 2002b).

19 In contrast to Cohen's preference for reciprocity in which each participant is *primarily* concerned about the outcome for the other party, consider Hayek's illuminating remark that, "we are independent of the will of those whose services we need because they use us for their own purposes and are normally little interested in the uses we make of their services. ... It is

largely because in the economic transactions of everyday life we are only impersonal means to our fellows, who help us for their own purposes, that we can count on such help from complete strangers and use it for whatever end we wish" (1960: 141).

20 Recall the slogan, cited in Chapter 3, note 16, "A price is a signal wrapped up in an incentive."

21 I say "*tax*-and-transfer" although Cohen seems to hope that the egalitarian dispositions of those who garner more than equal income will induce the voluntary surrender of their surplus receipts.

Bibliography

Ackerman, Bruce (1983) "On Getting What We Don't Deserve," *Social Philosophy and Policy* 1, 60–70.

Axelrod, Robert (1985) *The Evolution of Cooperation*. New York: Basic Books.

Bader, Ralf (2013) *Robert Nozick*. London: Bloombury Publishing.

Bader, Ralf (2017) "Counterfactual Justifications of the State," in David Sobel, Peter Vallentyne, and Steven Wall (eds.), *Oxford Studies in Political Philosophy, vol. 3*, pp. 101–31.

Barden, Garrett and Tim Murphy (2010) *Law and Justice in Community*. Oxford: Oxford University Press.

Barnett, Randy (2004) *Restoring the Lost Constitution*. Princeton, NJ: Princeton University Press.

Bastiat, Frederic (2012 [1848]) "The State," in *"The Law," "The State," and Other Political Writings* (David Hart, ed.). Indianapolis, IN: Liberty Fund.

Beito, David (2000) *From Mutual Aid to the Welfare State*. Chapel Hill, NC: University of North Carolina Press.

Benson, Bruce (2011) *The Enterprise of Law: Justice Without the State*. Oakland, CA: The Independent Institute.

Bicchieri, Cristina (2005) *The Grammar of Society*. Cambridge: Cambridge University Press.

Bosanquet, Bernard (2001 [1899]) *Philosophical Theory of the State* (William Sweet and Gerald Gaus, eds.). Bristol: Thoemnes Press.

Brennan, Jason (2014) *Why Not Capitalism?* New York: Routledge.

Bryan, Ben (2017) "The Conventionalist Challenge to Natural Rights Theory," *Social Practice and Theory* 43:3, 569–87.

Carens, Joseph (1981) *Equality, Moral Incentives, and the Market.* Chicago, IL: University of Chicago Press.

Chartier, Gary (2013) *Anarchy and Legal Order.* Cambridge: Cambridge University Press.

Childs, Roy (1994) *Liberty against Power* (Joan Kennedy Taylor, ed.). San Francisco, CA: Fox & Wilkes.

Childs, Roy (2007) "The Invisible Hand Strikes Back," in Edward Stringham (ed.), *Anarchy and the Law.* New Brunswick, NJ: Transaction Publishers, pp. 218–31.

Cohen, G. A. (1995) *Self-Ownership, Freedom, and Equality.* Cambridge: Cambridge University Press.

Cohen, G. A (2009) *Why Not Socialism?* Princeton, NJ: Princeton University Press.

Cowen, Tyler (2007) "Law as a Public Good: The Economics of Anarchy," in Edward Stringham (ed.), *Anarchy and the Law.* New Brunswick, NJ: Transaction Publishers, pp. 268–83.

Cowen, Tyler and Alex Tabarrok (2015) *Modern Principles of Microeconomics.* New York: Macmillan.

Epstein, Richard (2005) "One Step Beyond Nozick's Minimal State," *Social Philosophy and Policy* 22:1, 286–313.

Friedman, David (1973) *The Machinery of Freedom.* New York: Harper and Row.

Friedman, David (2007) "Law as a Private Good," in Edward Stringham (ed.), *Anarchy and the Law.* New Brunswick, NJ: Transaction Publishers, pp. 285–91.

Gaus, Gerald (2012) *The Order of Public Reason.* Cambridge: Cambridge University Press.

Gaus, Gerald (2015) "The Egalitarian Species," *Social Philosophy and Policy* 31:2, 1–27.

Gaus, Gerald (2016) *The Tyranny of the Ideal.* Princeton, NJ: Princeton University Press.

Gaus, Gerald (2017) "Hayek's 'Classical' Liberalism," in Jason Brennan, David Schmidtz, and Bas van der Vossen (eds.), *Routledge Handbook of Libertarianism.* New York: Routledge, pp. 34–52.

Hayek, F. A. (1944) *The Road to Serfdom.* Chicago, IL: University of Chicago Press.

Hayek, F. A. (1948 [1945]) "The Use of Knowledge in Society," in Hayek, *Individualism and Economic Order.* Chicago, IL: University of Chicago Press, pp. 77–91.

Hayek, F. A. (1948) *Individualism and Economic Order.* Chicago, IL: University of Chicago Press.

Hayek, F. A. (1960) *The Constitution of Liberty.* Chicago, IL: University of Chicago Press.

Hayek, F. A. (1964) *The Counter-Revolution of Science.* New York: Free Press.

Hayek, F. A. (1973) *Law, Legislation, and Liberty, vol. I, Rules and Order.* Chicago, IL: University of Chicago Press.

Hayek, F. A. (1976) *Law, Legislation, and Liberty, vol. II, The Mirage of Social Justice.* Chicago, IL: University of Chicago Press.

Hayek, F. A. (1979) *Law, Legislation, and Liberty, vol. III, The Political Order of a Free People.* Chicago, IL: University of Chicago Press.

Hayek, F. A. (1981) "Foreword," in Ludwig von Mises, *Socialism* (*Die Gemeinwirtschaft: Untersuchungen über den Sozialismus,* 1922). Indianapolis, IN: Liberty Fund, pp. xix–xxiv.

Hayek, F. A. (1988) *The Fatal Conceit.* Chicago, IL: University of Chicago Press.

Hayek, F. A. (1997 [1939]) "Freedom and the Economic System," in *The Collected Works of F. A. Hayek, volume 10* (Bruce Caldwell, ed.). Chicago, IL: University of Chicago Press, pp. 189–211.

Huemer, Michael (2013) *The Problem of Political Obligation.* New York: Palgrave Macmillan.

Hume, David (1985) "Of the Original Contract," in *Essays Moral, Political, and Literary* (Eugene Miller, ed.). Indianapolis, IN: Liberty Fund, pp. 465–87.

Hume, David (2000 [1740]) *A Treatise of Human Nature. Book III On Morals* (David Norton and Mary Norton, eds.). Oxford: Oxford University Press.

Leeson, Peter (2014) *Anarchy Unbound.* Cambridge: Cambridge University Press.

Lippmann, Walter (1937) *An Inquiry into the Principles of a Good Society.* Boston, MA: Little, Brown and Co.

Locke, John (1959 [1689]) *An Essay Concerning Human Understanding* (A. C. Fraser, ed.). New York: Dover.

Locke, John (1960 [1689]) *Two Treatises of Government* (Peter Laslett, ed.). Cambridge: Cambridge University Press.

Locke, John (1980 [1689]) *Second Treatise of Government* (C. B. Macpherson, ed.). Indianapolis, IN: Hackett Publishing.

Locke, John (1983 [1689]) *A Letter Concerning Toleration* (James Tully, ed.). Indianapolis, IN: Hackett Publishing.

Locke, John (1997a) *Locke: Political Essays* (Mark Goldie, ed.). Cambridge: Cambridge University Press.

Locke, John (1997b) "Essays on the Law of Nature," in *Locke: Political Essays* (Mark Goldie, ed.). Cambridge: Cambridge University Press, pp. 79–113.

Locke, John (1997c) "An Essay on Toleration," in *Locke: Political*

Essays (Mark Goldie, ed.). Cambridge: Cambridge University Press, pp. 134–59.

Locke, John (1997d) "Thus, I Think," in *Locke: Political Essays* (Mark Goldie, ed.). Cambridge: Cambridge University Press, p. 296.

Lomasky, Loren (1987) *Persons, Rights, and the Moral Community.* Oxford: Oxford University Press.

Lomasky, Loren and Fernando Teson (2015) *Justice at a Distance.* Cambridge: Cambridge University Press.

Mack, Eric (1989) "Moral Individualism: Agent-Relativity and Deontic Restraints," *Social Philosophy and Policy* 7:1, 81–111.

Mack, Eric (1990) "Self-Ownership and the Right of Property," *The Monist* 73:4, 519–43.

Mack, Eric (1995) "The Self-Ownership Proviso: A New and Improved Lockean Proviso," *Social Philosophy and Policy* 12:1, 186–218.

Mack, Eric (2000a) "Self-Ownership, Marxism, and Egalitarianism: Part I," *Politics, Philosophy, and Economics* 1:1, 75–108.

Mack, Eric (2000b) "Self-Ownership, Marxism, and Egalitarianism: Part II," *Politics, Philosophy, and Economics* 1:2, 237–76.

Mack, Eric (2006a) "Non-Absolute Rights and Libertarian Taxation," *Social Philosophy and Policy* 23:2, 109–41.

Mack, Eric (2006b) "Hayek on Justice and the Order of Actions," in Edward Feser (ed.), *Cambridge Companion to Hayek.* Cambridge: Cambridge University Press, pp. 259–86.

Mack, Eric (2009) "What is Left in Left-Libertarianism?," in Stephen de Wijze, Matthew H. Kramer, and Ian Carter (eds.), *Hillel Steiner and the Anatomy of Justice.* London: Routledge, pp. 101–31.

Mack, Eric (2010) "The Natural Right of Property," *Social Philosophy and Policy* 27, 53–78.

Mack, Eric (2011) "Nozickian Arguments for the More-Than-Minimal State," in Ralf Bader and John Meadowcroft (eds.), *Cambridge Companion to Anarchy, State, and Utopia.* Cambridge: Cambridge University Press, pp. 89–115.

Mack, Eric (2013) *John Locke.* New York: Bloomsbury Academic.

Mack, Eric (2014) "Robert Nozick's Political Philosophy," *Stanford Encyclopedia of Philosophy.* Available at: http://plato.stanford.edu/entries/nozick-political (accessed on January 15, 2017).

Mack, Eric (2015) "Elbow Room for Rights," in David Sobel, Peter Vallentyne, and Steven Wall (eds.), *Oxford Studies in Political Philosophy, vol. 1.* Oxford: Oxford University Press, pp. 194–221.

Mack, Eric (2016) "Elbow Room for Self-Defense," *Social Philosophy and Policy* 32:2, 18–39.

Mack, Eric (2017) "What is Seen and What is Not Seen," *Georgetown Journal of Law and Public Policy* 15, 811–34.

Mack, Eric and Gerald Gaus (2004) "Classical Liberalism and Libertarianism: The Liberty Tradition," in Gerald Gaus and Chandran Kukathus (eds.), *A Handbook of Political Theory*. London: Routledge, pp. 115–30.

Mill, John Stuart (1960 [1873]) *Autobiography of John Stuart Mill*. New York: Columbia University Press.

Mill, John Stuart (1978 [1859]) *On Liberty* (Elizabeth Rapaport, ed.). Indianapolis, IN: Hackett Publishing.

Mill, John Stuart (2000 [1863]) *Utilitarianism*. Peterborough, ON: Broadview Press.

Mill, John Stuart (2006 [1848]) *Principles of Political Economy* (J. M. Robson, ed.). Indianapolis, IN: Liberty Fund.

Mill, John Stuart (2006) "The Difficulties of Socialism," in *Essays on Economics and Society* (J. M. Robson, ed.). Toronto: Toronto University Press, pp. 737–49.

Mises, Ludwig von (1981 [1922]) *Socialism* (*Die Gemeinwirtschaft: Untersuchungen über den Sozialismus*). Indianapolis, IN: Liberty Fund.

Murphy, Liam and Thomas Nagel (2002) *The Myth of Ownership*. Oxford: Oxford University Press.

Nagel, Thomas (1981) "Libertarianism without Foundations," in Jeffrey Paul (ed.), *Reading Nozick*. Totowa, NJ: Rowman and Littlefield, pp. 191–205.

Narveson, Jan (1988) *The Libertarian Idea*. Philadelphia, PA: Temple University Press.

Narveson, Jan (2017) "Contractarianism," in Aaron Powell and Grant Babcock (eds.), *Arguments for Liberty*. Washington, DC: Cato Institute, pp. 123–60.

Nozick, Robert (1974) *Anarchy, State, and Utopia*. New York: Basic Books.

Nozick, Robert (2001) *Invariances*. Cambridge, MA: Harvard University Press.

Ostrom, Elinor (1990) *Governing the Commons*. Cambridge: Cambridge University Press.

Powell, Aaron and Grant Babcock (eds.) (2017) *Arguments for Liberty*. Washington, DC: Cato Institute.

Raico, Ralph (2002) "Robert Nozick: A Historical Note." Available at: https://archive.lewrockwell.com/raico/raico15.html (accessed on July 1, 2017).

Rand, Ayn (1957) *Atlas Shrugged*. New York: New American Library.

Rand, Ayn (1964a) "The Nature of Government," in *The Virtue of Selfishness*. New York: New American Library, pp. 125–34.

Rand, Ayn (1964b) "Government Financing in a Free Society," in *The Virtue of Selfishness*. New York: New American Library, pp. 135–40.

Rasmussen, Douglas and Douglas Den Uyl (1991) *Liberty and Nature: An Aristotelian Defense of Liberal Order*. LaSalle, IL: Open Court.

Rasmussen, Douglas and Douglas Den Uyl (2005) *Norms of Liberty*. University Park, PA: Pennsylvania State University Press.

Rasmussen, Douglas and Douglas Den Uyl (2006) "The Myth of Atomism," *The Review of Metaphysics* 59, 841–68.

Rasmussen, Douglas and Douglas Den Uyl (2016) *The Perfectionist Turn*. Edinburgh: Edinburgh University Press.

Rawls, John (1971) *A Theory of Justice*. Cambridge, MA: Harvard University Press.

Rawls, John (1993) *Political Liberalism*. Cambridge, MA: Harvard University Press.

Rothbard, Murray (1973) *For a New Liberty*. New York: Macmillan.

Rothbard, Murray (1974) "Anatomy of the State," in Roy Childs (ed.), *Egalitarianism as a Revolt Against Nature*. Washington, DC: Libertarian Review Press, pp. 55–88.

Rothbard, Murray (1978) "Society without a State," in J. Roland Pennock and John W. Chapman (eds.), *Anarchism*. New York: New York University Press, pp. 191–207.

Rothbard, Murray (2007) "Robert Nozick and the Immaculate Conception of the State," in Edward Stringham (ed.), *Anarchy and the Law*. New Brunswick, NJ: Transaction Publishers, pp. 233–49.

Russell, Daniel (2010) "Embodiment and Self-Ownership," *Social Philosophy and Policy* 27, 135–67.

Schmidtz, David (1994) "The Institution of Property," *Social Philosophy and Policy* 11, 42–62.

Schmidtz, David (1995) *Rational Choice and Moral Agency*. Princeton, NJ: Princeton University Press.

Schmidtz, David (1998) "Taking Responsibility" in David Schmidtz and Robert Goodin (eds.), *Social Welfare and Individual Responsibility*. Cambridge: Cambridge University Press, pp. 1–96.

Schmidtz, David (ed.) (2002) *Robert Nozick*. Cambridge: Cambridge University Press.

Schmidtz, David (2006) *Elements of Justice*. Cambridge: Cambridge University Press.

Schmidtz, David (2011) "Nonideal Theory: What It Is and What It Needs to Be," *Ethics* 121:1, 772–96.

Smart, J. J. C. (1973) "An Outline of a System of Utilitarian Ethics," in J. J. C. Smart and Bernard Williams, *Utilitarianism: For and Against*. Cambridge: Cambridge University Press, pp. 1–74.

Smith, Adam (1981 [1776]) *An Inquiry into the Nature and Causes of the Wealth of Nations* (R. H. Campbell and A. S. Skinner, eds.). Indianapolis, IN: Liberty Fund.

Spencer, Herbert (1970 [1851]) *Social Statics*. New York: Robert Schalkenbach Foundation.

Spooner, Lysander (1973 [1870]) *No Treason: The Constitution of No Authority*. Colorado Springs, CO: Ralph Myles Publisher.

Steiner, Hillel (1976) "The Natural Right to the Means of Production," *Philosophical Quarterly* 27, 41–9.

Steiner, Hillel (1977) "The Structure of a Set of Compossible Rights," *Journal of Philosophy* lxxiv, 767–75.

Steiner, Hillel (1994) *An Essay on Rights*. Oxford: Blackwell.

Steiner, Hillel (2006) "Self-Ownership and Conscription," in Christine Sypnowich (ed.), *The Egalitarian Conscience*. Oxford: Oxford University Press, pp. 88–101.

Steiner, Hillel (2009) "Left Libertarianism and the Ownership of Natural Resources," *Public Reason* 1, 1–8.

Tabarrok, Alex (2015) "A Price is a Signal Wrapped Up in an Incentive." Available at: http://marginalrevolution.com/marginalrevolution/2015/02/a-price-is-signal-wrapped-up-in-an-incentive.html (accessed on March 15, 2017).

Tannehill, Morris and Linda Tannehill (1972) *The Market for Liberty*. New York: Arno Press.

Trevor-Roper, Hugh (1967) *The Crisis of the Seventeen Century*. Indianapolis, IN: Liberty Fund.

Tucker, Benjamin (1972 [1893]) *Instead of a Book*. New York: Arno Press.

Vallier, Kevin (2017) "Rawlsianism," in Aaron Powell and Grant Babcock (eds.), *Arguments for Liberty*. Washington, DC: Cato Institute, pp. 161–202.

Waldron, Jeremy (ed.) (1987) *Nonsense on Stilts*. London: Methuen.

Williams, Bernard (1973) "A Critique of Utilitarianism," in J. J. C. Smart and Bernard Williams, *Utilitarianism: For and Against*. Cambridge: Cambridge University Press, pp. 75–150.

Index

Page numbers in italics are for the Online Chapter, "Further Philosophical Roads to Libertarianism"